Song and Self

THE RANDY L. AND MELVIN R. BERLIN
FAMILY LECTURES

Song & Self

A Singer's Reflections on
Music and Performance

Ian Bostridge

The University of Chicago Press
CHICAGO

The University of Chicago Press, Chicago 60637
© 2023 by Ian Bostridge
All rights reserved. No part of this book may be used or reproduced in any
manner whatsoever without written permission, except in the case of brief
quotations in critical articles and reviews. For more information, contact the
University of Chicago Press, 1427 E. 60th St., Chicago, IL 60637.
Published 2023
Printed in the United States of America

32 31 30 29 28 27 26 25 24 23   1 2 3 4 5

ISBN-13: 978-0-226-80948-9 (cloth)
ISBN-13: 978-0-226-82294-5 (e-book)
DOI: https://doi.org/10.7208/chicago/9780226822945.001.0001

The University of Chicago Press gratefully acknowledges the generous support
of the Division of the Humanities at the University of Chicago toward the
publication of this book.

Lines quoted from *Four Quartets* by permission of the T. S. Eliot estate and
HarperCollins US.

Library of Congress Cataloging-in-Publication Data

Names: Bostridge, Ian, author.
Title: Song and self : a singer's reflections on music and performance / Ian
Bostridge.
Other titles: Randy L. and Melvin R. Berlin family lectures.
Description: Chicago : University of Chicago Press, 2023. | Series: Randy L. and
Melvin R. Berlin family lectures | Includes bibliographical references and
index.
Identifiers: LCCN 2022026742 | ISBN 9780226809489 (cloth) |
ISBN 9780226822945 (ebook)
Subjects: LCSH: Vocal music—History and criticism. | Britten, Benjamin, 1913–
1976. Vocal music. | Ravel, Maurice, 1875–1937. Chansons madécasses. |
Gender identity in music. | Death in music. | Vocal music—Political
aspects—Europe—History.
Classification: LCC ML1600 .B67 2023 | DDC 782.109—dc23/eng/20220615
LC record available at https://lccn.loc.gov/2022026742

♾ This paper meets the requirements of ANSI/NISO Z39.48-1992
(Permanence of Paper).

To Lucasta, il miglior fabbro

So I assumed a double part, and cried
And heard another's voice cry: "What! are you here?"

T. S. ELIOT, "Little Gidding"

Identities are never unified and, in late modern times, increasingly fragmented and fractured; never singular but multiply constructed across different, often intersecting and antagonistic, discourses, practices, and positions. They are subject to a radical historicization, and are constantly in the process of change and transformation. . . . Identities are therefore constituted within, not outside representation.

STUART HALL, "Who Needs 'Identity'"

Contents

Preface

These essays started life as lectures, the Berlin Family Lectures at the University of Chicago, and I would like to start by expressing my thanks to the Berlin family and the University of Chicago for the invitation. It has been a precious opportunity to reflect. As a singer, I spent much of 2020 and 2021 unable to perform live music because of the COVID-19 pandemic. To that extent, like all performers worldwide, I have been forced to question an identity, a self, that has, for the past twenty or thirty years, been defined by getting up on stage and communicating music in physical proximity and real time to audiences in concert halls and opera houses.

I have had an unusual career in that before I became a professional singer in my late twenties I was an academic historian. The enforced silence of the last year has given me the opportunity to fall back on my identity as a historian and to think. It has given me the chance to delve deeper than I might otherwise have had the time to do into the backstories of some of the works of classical music that I have performed in the past, or have been thinking about performing in the future, by composers ranging from the Italian Renaissance (Claudio Monteverdi) to twentieth-century Britain (Benjamin Britten).

In these essays I will venture on a journey under the surface of those works, share my excavations, and ask questions about them that are not usually asked in the concert hall. The tradition of Western classical music, far from being moribund or culturally authoritarian, continues to be alive because it continually invites us to ask questions. The individual musical works I will explore prove to be fluid and open-ended while at the same time making us emotionally engage with the conflicts and contradictions of human experience—including power relations, whether gendered or colonial, and the way we confront the ultimate dissolution of self, death, something that has been at the forefront of our minds during a year and more of global pandemic. Music, at its best, embodies with peculiar force what the poet John Keats called "negative capability," the creative ability to live with doubts and mysteries. It makes us think and at the same time it takes us beyond thought.

The question(ing) of identity is the starting point of these essays, but they remain essays: provisional, experimental, suggestive. They do not set out a thesis; they have no agenda. Improvisatory rather than systematically theorized, they aim to reveal or underline complexity, to add texture, to problematize. Drawing instinctively on my practice as a performer, I come to these issues not as a philosopher or social theorist but with a sense that personal identity is somehow formed out of an encounter between the self and what is outside the self; that it is both culturally constructed and inflected by intuitive subjectivity. If identity is in part performative, these essays are, in turn, offered as an open-ended performance in which I invite readers—the audience—to respond to their different strands, their themes and variations, as they would perhaps to a piece of music itself.

The first essay explores the ways in which vocal pieces by Monteverdi, Schumann, and Britten—none of them straightforwardly operatic—can blur the boundaries of gender. In the second essay, I research the historical and political roots of a single song by Ravel from his *Chansons madécasses* (*Songs of Madagascar*) that has always both haunted and unnerved me. I hope to deepen and inform our response to it, to use it to reflect upon the past and the present by exploring its ambiguous and often disturbing context and the way it constructs and deconstructs colonial and "othered" identities. I end with death in the third essay because death is the end of everything, because music speaks to death, and because death is the absence in the face of which all human identity is constructed.

⊢

In all performance, identity is something that we performers have to confront. We play a "double part." Each time we stand up on stage to deliver, to reproduce, to transmit a text, be it musical or literary or a combination of the two, we have a decision to make (conscious or unconscious) about the character of that text and about the stance we adopt towards it. How are we, quite literally, to embody it? Do we take on the identity of the text we have absorbed, or does the text reconfigure itself as it is molded to the identity of the performer? There are many ways of approaching this, and many orthodoxies that are, sometimes unthinkingly, lodged at the center of critical discourse.

Central to much appreciation of the Western art music tradition is the idea of "interpretation," but interpretation understood as a part shamanic, part scientific quest for the "right" performance. It's a strange notion, and one we don't apply in quite the same way to the spoken theater. A great actor's "interpretation" of Macbeth, Hedda Gabler, or Archie Rice is simply his or her performance. The actor takes the text and runs with it, and the performance that results is not typically a search for something legitimate or authoritative. *Interpres* in Latin is the agent between two parties, a broker or negotiator. A performance in the spoken theater is a negotiation between text and actors.

In classical music there is a paradox at work in which the ideal interpretation is, essentially, a noninterpretation. There has long been a tendency rather to privilege the text, in this case the musical score, a tendency that reached its apogee in twentieth-century abstract music with the notion that the performer is an ideally transparent individual. Composers like Stravinsky hoped, through notational exactitude, to remove the freedom of the performer; not for nothing did he experiment with the mechanical piano roll in the 1920s as a way of escaping the painful necessity for the intermediation of a performer.[1] Interpretation, understood in this way, is about taking the text left behind by the composer and using it to intuit an ideal performance that remains unachievable but that is nevertheless an absolute regulatory principle and an aspiration. Much time in rehearsal is spent arguing about what the composer "meant" (though in practice quite often ignoring it). The ultimate expression of this regime was articulated by the theorist Heinrich Schenker (1868–1935): "Basically a composition does not require a performance in order to exist. ... The reading of the score is sufficient."[2] There's something profoundly theological about this, as it reaches back to Renaissance debates about form and substance, but it is surely a kick in the teeth for the performer.

The classical singer stands somehow, and a little awkwardly, between these two poles. For an opera singer, the demands of the theater and a theatrical attitude of mind largely predominate. An opera singer is an actor. In the concert repertoire, and more particularly in the field of song, things are more confused, and there is often a demand or a felt need to avoid dramatization, a self-denying ordinance in the service of some idea of an uninterpreted, natural delivery, which somehow connects to Stravinsky's suspicion of expressivity in classical music. This notion of a natural delivery is, of course, a myth—all art is artifice—but the debate on how to deliver song goes right back to Schubert's day.

Thankfully, a new performative turn in musicology has been recognizing that music, quite simply, is performance, not just the written text.[3] Music is a quintessentially social activity. Of course, in our highly literate tradition of classical music making, the composer has a unique power, authority, and charisma, and the technologies of music composition and the genius of the composers who have used and developed them have created a tradition of extraordinary power and longevity, from Monteverdi via Mozart and Beethoven to Ades. At the same time, performers, all performers, like actors, have to take the music and run with it. The text we have cannot exhaustively encode all the parameters of possible performances, and while the text may be the starting point, and research into its meanings a useful and constraining discipline, in the end what we have is a recipe for making performances that, in one way or another, move our audiences.

This is, in fact, as much the case for instrumental music as it is for vocal music in the classical tradition. In a brilliant essay the pianist Alfred Brendel contends that in the piano music of Beethoven, over and above the analysis and deployment of structure, "it is the interpreter's responsibility to play the roles of different characters."[4] If this is the case for abstract music of the highest intellectual charge, how much more so for sung music, for music that has a literary text and assumes if not a literal character—as in works for the theater—at least a persona, as in the world of song.

Here is Edward T. Cone in his classic study, *The Composer's Voice*:

> If we take the art of song seriously, we must accord the same faith to the characters portrayed by singers. They are not mere puppets, controlled by the composer's strings. They are more like Petrouchkas, brought to life by the composer, but thenceforth driven by their own wills and desires. Thus the vocal persona adopts the original simulation of the poetic persona and adds another of his own[5]

Singers are not puppets, Cone says, with his ironic nod towards Stravinsky; and he is surely right. The adoption of character, the merging of the characters of both piece and performer that performance involves can often take us a long way from what a composer "intended." At the same time, one of the most powerful feelings one can have as a performer is that in what feel like the best, the "deepest" performances—for the singer, and with an assumption that this is felt by the audience too—the song sings the singer. If this sounds a little mystagogical, it is an idea that nevertheless does capture, phenomenologically as it were, what it feels like to deliver a work of art and to be swept along with it, taken by surprise by the way it seizes us and takes us unaware. Moments in life like this are rare, moments of uncanniness in which parts of our life seem to connect in a jolting and mysterious way, moments of what we might call epiphany. Art seeks out such epiphanies, and for the singer and their audience they come when the song sings the singer.

I wanted to talk about this confrontation, this adventure with identity, because over the course of the past thirty years as a singer, I have found myself torn between two approaches that seem, at first sight, to be contradictory. Educated as a historian and having worked as a university-based historian until the age of thirty, my musical life was always outside this academic structure. I never learned to play an instrument, I never studied harmony and counterpoint. Singing the Romantic songs of Schubert, Schumann, Brahms, and Wolf, my self-legitimation did not come from an academic understanding of the poetico-musical texts that I loved and sang but from a commitment to a sort of intensity of utterance and that search to be so immersed in the music that singer and song merge. My singerly practice was never about transparency but about merger and that paradoxical escape from the self that a certain intensity of performance can bring.

At the same time, I recognized—as a historian—the way in which the music I was singing had emerged from different cultural moments in the history of the Western classical tradition and that each, perhaps, deserved excavation as to the way in which character might be understood. If one's first extensive encounter with sung performance is the Romantic lied, then the performative style one adopts is all too likely, of course, to be a Romantic one. Recognition of the historical roots of that style can't disqualify it as an artistic approach. I'm reminded of the twentieth-century British composer Benjamin Britten, who declared that if he had been born a hundred years earlier he would have been a Romantic composer—something he meant not as a statement of the obvious but as a declaration of allegiance. It was Nietzsche who told us that every song is a swan song.[6] For me, every song is, somehow, Romantic, and involves an engagement with the themes of life that the Romantics explored and transmitted into the psychoanalytic tradition: Eros and Thanatos, love and death; identity, or, more simply, who are we, who am I?

In these essays I want to look at a selection of diverse pieces that might benefit from having their presentation of identity problematized and historicized. It's my conviction that this is both a practical and a moral issue. We owe it to both the past and to the present to understand the context from which art emerges, as part of that mysterious creative current that attempts to bind together in cultural catholicity the dead, the living, and the as yet unborn. I want to examine performative constructions of identity in music through the lens of gender, politics, or the ultimate paradoxical grounding and denial of identity, death. Works that seem difficult for us to perform, like Robert Schumann's Romantic song cycle *Frauenliebe und Leben*, can be reimagined by taking a closer look at their origins. Works that have languished in an ideological exile like Ravel's *Chansons madécasses* are not just aesthetic objects, for Ravel's song cycle exists in a historical matrix that both opposes and is complicit in the European colonial enterprise. In these essays I will be looking at pieces that I have performed or that I might perform. In doing so, I want to raise questions, questions that help the past to inform the present, the present to inform the past, and that can enrich as well as interrogate performance.

1
Blurring Identities

Gender in Performance

This essay considers three works from three different eras to look at the way in which one aspect of social identity—that of gender identity—has been creatively reconfigured by composers and performers at particular historical moments. Questions of gender have been recurring sites of complexity within the European musical tradition. Musical works can provide an open and fluid space in which societies can pose such questions.

The late-Renaissance short theatrical piece by Claudio Monteverdi, *Il combattimento di Tancredi e Clorinda* (1624), depicts the fight between Tancredi and Clorinda. Complexities of identity are presented through the telling of a tale in which gender roles are blurred and challenged. In Robert Schumann's song cycle *Frauenliebe und Leben* (1840), the Romantic and romanticized presentation of a woman's life and love is complicated by the male identity of its authors, composer and poet. Closer to us, in Benjamin Britten's music theater piece *Curlew River* (1964), the blurring of gender—more specifically, the assumption of a female role by a male singer—broadens and deepens the vein of tragedy in the piece.

Monteverdi's musical theater works, written in the first few decades of the seventeenth century, are now firmly lodged in the repertoire. But standing at the beginning of the opera tradition, before firm rules for what an opera should be had been codified, they are fluid works, strange and unsettling for a modern audience. They must have been strange and unsettling for Monteverdi's contemporaries. *L'Orfeo*, written for the Gonzaga Duke of Mantua in 1607, is more of a court entertainment than an opera. Nowadays it is usually in opera houses that it is to be seen and heard. Despite all the philosophical and musicological conundrums and paradoxes about what it is to recreate a work written four centuries ago—what is authenticity, how can we approach it?—it has that strange amphibious quality of seeming at one and the same time both alien and familiar. It mixes together emotions that are recognizable and emotions that seem barely to engage with our concerns. This is what music of the past seems to do for us, to bring the foreignness and the humanity of the past to life with a visceral impact, far away from what some commentators dismiss as classical music's "museum" culture.

Monteverdi's Venetian operas *Il ritorno d'Ulisse in patria* (1639/40) and *L'incoronazione di Poppea* (1643) are much more operatic in feel, much more obviously designed for a theater and for a public. They are freewheeling, with that almost Shakespearean mixture of the serious and the unbuttoned that reminds us that these pieces were written for the carnival season, in which the social and ideological assumptions of the Venetian Republic could be seen as it were through a gaudy theatrical kaleidoscope, the world turned upside down. Another carnival piece by Monteverdi is even more difficult to categorize, though it is increasingly a part of the postmodern classical repertoire. *Il combattimento di Tancredi e Clorinda*, or *The Fight between Tancredi and Clorinda*, was written to be performed as part of some evening entertainments in the apartments of the Mocenigo family in the Palazzo Dandolo on Venice's fabled Riva degli Schiavoni at the height of carnival in 1624. The basic story line is a simple one, but at the same time it challenges the tropes of heteronormativity. During the First Crusade a Muslim warrior is trapped outside the gates of Jerusalem and is challenged by the Christian knight Tancredi. They fight. Tancredi demands to know who his opponent is. Meeting with a refusal, he is spurred on to further, furious combat. As the fighting intensifies Tancredi mortally wounds his opponent, who asks him to administer baptism. As he makes to do so, he finally recognizes his enemy as Clorinda—the woman he loves. She dies.

Combattimento has an experimental quality about it, and at the time of that first performance, it must have packed an avant-garde punch, as a group of singers, instrumentalists, and actor-dancers started, in the middle of a party, to enact Torquato Tasso's story. The killing of Clorinda by Tancredi, in a domestic setting, close up, must have lent the climax an especially disturbing frisson. Here is Monteverdi's own description of the evening:

> Unexpectedly [and that's crucial for the impact of the evening] Clorinda enters, armed and on foot. She is followed by Tancredi, armed, on a Marian horse [some sort of hobby horse?] The narrator, Testo, begins the singing.... Tancredi and Clorinda will perform steps and gestures in the way expressed by the narration, nothing more or less, and they will observe diligently those measures,

blows and steps from the players. The instrumentalists will sound excited or soft, and the narrator will deliver the words set to music, in such a way that they create a unified imitation.[1]

Monteverdi's setting of this incident out of Tasso must have had a peculiarly dissociated feeling. The narrator is designated Testo, literally "text," but a common label for a narrator or soloist in Italian music. He spins his tale while two actor-dancers act out the combat. At four crucial points of the drama, Tancredi and Clorinda themselves are given voice— but did the actors sing or did they mime as the characters sing their own words? It is not clear.

Monteverdi was especially proud of his development of new musical means to depict combat in sound, something he boasted of in the preface to the work as published in 1639. Pizzicati, rapid repeated notes, string tremolos: this was what he called the *concitato genere*, the aroused style, which imitates the sounds of combat. But what seems particularly notable, hearing and seeing the work today, is the sexual charge of the material from Tasso that Monteverdi set. The aroused style may originate in imitations of the warlike, but its signifying potential can just as easily attach to a very different sort of arousal.

In true carnivalesque style, *Combattimento* plays with notions of gender, emphasizing the fluidity and performativity of gender roles. And the fight between the two combatants is full of erotic ambiguity. The elite audience for the first performance would surely have been well aware of Tasso's poem and its complex presentation of the relationship between Tancredi and Clorinda.

Tancredi first sees Clorinda early on in the poem, falls in love with her, and refuses to fight her. Clorinda herself nurses a secret desire for Tancredi. In an often overlooked passage from canto 3, she is presented as an active and almost predatory sexual actor, a challenge to the Renaissance norm, and one who "concealed under the cloak of hate another passion":

Oh that I might have
That man my captive, and alive not dead—
Alive I want him for a sweet revenge
So my desires may yet be comforted.

When the two meet again in canto 12, Clorinda has put on armor, which conceals her identity and her sex from Tancredi, and fights him, adopting a masculine persona that Tancredi fails to see through. In the passage set by Monteverdi, the encounter is as much an erotic as a martial one, and combat is reimagined as a display of sadomasochistic lovemaking:

Three times the knight gripped the young lady hard
In his muscular arms, and three times she
Slipped herself out of those tenacious knots
No true love's, but the bonds of an enemy.

Here Monteverdi's music irradiates the words with a syncopated sliding lovesickness.

When Tancredi comes to kill Clorinda, there is something disturbingly erotic about Tasso's words, heightened by the sheer simplicity of Monteverdi's setting:

Into her lovely breast he thrusts his blade,
Drowns it, eagerly drinks her blood. Her stole
Beneath the cuirass, sweetly lined with gold,
That held her breasts with light and tender pull,
Now fills with a warm stream.

5

The story ends with Clorinda asking Tancredi to baptize her with water from a nearby stream, with his devastated recognition of her—a moment captured in Tintoretto's magnificent painting of the subject, now in Houston—and her reported Christian redemption (plate 1).[2]

Who is Clorinda? In a seventeenth-century Venetian context, as the historian Wendy Heller has explored, the role and character of women was a matter for constant negotiation and debate—mostly, of course, by men. This was a polity in which women were excluded from political power even more resolutely than in other Italian states of the time, where the institution of the court did at least allow for the play of informal female influence. The marriage customs of the republic, designed to safeguard the transmission of property, condemned many, if not most, unmarried aristocratic women to an unchosen life encloistered as a nun.[3]

But women did write about the constraints under which they lived, none more eloquently than Lucrezia Marinella (1571–1653) in her "La nobiltà et l'eccelenza dell donne co' difetti et mancamenti de gli uomini" (The nobility and excellence of women together with the defects and insufficiencies of men):

> O that God might grant that in our times women were permitted to train in arms and in literature, so that we would see such wonderful and unheard-of things in the preservation and expansion of kingdoms. And who would be more ready to make a shield with their fearless breasts in defence of the fatherland than women?[4]

There were during the Renaissance rare but notable examples of such martial women: Elizabeth I confronting the

Spanish Armada in 1588 is perhaps the most famous—"not so much a virgin as a virago," as one contemporary put it, "in nought unlike the Amazonian queen," Penthesilea.[5] Tasso himself was particularly proud that in his epic he managed to include the Amazonian warrior Clorinda, as Homer had not managed to represent the Amazonian Queen Penthesilea in his *Iliad*. Yet at the same time, she was a *finta persona*, a marvel, and for Tasso there were clear gender roles to which men and women, under normal conditions, ought to conform—strength, commerce, and combat for men, modesty and household management for women.[6]

In a sense Tancredi's performance of heteronormative male gender is put into question as much by *Combattimento* as is Clorinda's. The erotic quality of the combat is multilayered, tangled, perplexing. Clorinda loves Tancredi—without quite knowing how or why—and fights with him to the death in order, somehow, to possess him. Tancredi is all unknowing of Clorinda's identity as a woman but joins in this sensual combat with a feigning man. When she is revealed to be a woman—and, what is more, the woman with whom he is in love—his sense of masculine identity is cast adrift, a moment of crisis for him. As for Clorinda, her agency is asserted by the piece—she insists on her confrontation with Tancredi, she pursues him—but she is ultimately punished for that agency by defeat and death; her carnival existence as a performative marvel is a licensed exception that only reinforces the mores and customs of Venetian society. What the gentlemen and gentlewomen who watched the first performance talked about after it we shall, of course, never know. We do know, however, from Monteverdi's own, possibly self-serving account, that tears were shed.

Combattimento is rich, almost too rich in its text and contexts, to contend with as a performer. A scholarly literature of formidable depth and suggestiveness has grown up around it. The audience watching in the 1620s would have been well aware from their steeping in Tasso—as a modern audience is not aware—that Clorinda, the white-skinned Muslim, was in fact the child of black-skinned Ethiopian Christian royalty, another confusion of identity that would have given her baptism a particular force, especially for Venetians who, living on a boundary between the Christian and Islamic worlds, would have known stories of Venetians brought up as Muslims, Ottomans brought up as Christians.[7] Suzanne Cusick has uncovered fascinating possibilities of sexual double entendre at work in the text Monteverdi sets, creating the prospect of layers of carnivalesque tension between the planes of battle, of love, and of ribald jest.[8]

How does *Combattimento* work for performers in performance? I most recently sang it on tour, in concert, with the Italian original instrument orchestra Europa Galante under their director Fabio Biondi. As is so often the case nowadays, I sang the whole thing, the nameless narrator, Clorinda, and Tancredi, not Monteverdi's original design. In this version Testo is a ballad singer on stage telling a tale, an age old tale, but entering seamlessly into the roles within the story, and not only when Tancredi and Clorinda speak but also as the musical narration embodies the experiences of the combatants: aggression, desire, surrender. Clorinda's performativity as she pretends to be what she is not is echoed in the narrator's performance. It is a remarkably absorbing piece for performers and audience, given in this way, belying its fractured structure and the many commentators who see it as an aesthetic oddity. And in its exploration of the fluidity of gender and sexuality, of its fantastical imaginings, *Combattimento* is far more interesting than Monteverdi told his public when he boasted in the first edition of how cleverly he had mimicked the sounds of war. So much more is going on. *Combattimento* ends on a note of uncertainty. As she dies Clorinda only "seems" to say, according to the narration— "the heavens open, I go in peace." This openness, this absence of a conclusive happy ending, is echoed in a fractured cadence, a sort of disconnect between Clorinda's ending and that of the players, a resolution that comes disconcertingly after her sainted demise.[9]

                                   ⊢

Robert Schumann's song cycle for voice and piano, *Frauenliebe und Leben*, is a very different beast from Monteverdi's *Combattimento*. It inhabits the world of the Romantic lied. One of the most prestigious classical genres of the nineteenth century, the lied was virtually invented by Franz Schubert in the course of his short life. Piano and voice conspire to present a psychologically convincing persona, one with psychoanalytical pre-echoes: the voice speaks in conscious mode while the piano melds together the external world and the unconscious in waves of emotional yearning, a world away from the performative identities of the late Renaissance.

Frauenliebe is an extraordinarily compelling and moving piece of music. In the course of seven songs and twenty minutes we are witness to the experiences of a young woman who falls in love, marries, becomes pregnant, nurses her baby, and is widowed. If we only had a bare title for each song and no words to understand the detail, we would nevertheless still feel the emotional compulsion of the work, as we do with Schumann's wordless but literary piano cycles of the 1830s. The work closes with a meditative but devastating postlude

9

in the shadow of the husband's death. The music of the first song of the cycle, that first encounter with the beloved ("Seit ich ihn gesehen, glaub ich blind zu sein") returns, but with the vocal melody at first veiled and then vanishing, leaving only a memory in the mind of the listener. Charles Rosen, pianist and one of the great writers about music, has analyzed the subtle power of this supreme evocation of memory in music:

> The postlude is a memory, and part of the memory is missing: it has to be recalled, willed to return—as it inevitably is. Schumann has forced the listener to acknowledge the eternal imperfection of memory and to complete the song. The end of the cycle is not a return but the ghost of a return, a fragment or shadow of the original. The voice no longer exists, and with it has died part of the melody.[10]

Frauenliebe remains one of the most frequently performed of the song cycles of the Romantic period. Partly because of its sheer affective power, because of its innovative and compelling recreation of a domestic tragedy. Partly because it is one of the few song cycles with a poetic persona that is definitively female. But *Frauenliebe* is also something of an embarrassment today because of the nature of the texts, which seem to inhabit a world of nineteenth-century paternalism that twenty-first-century singers and twenty-first-century audiences find uncomfortable. It doesn't always seem to be easy to receive the songs, historically or dramatically, as the presentation of a world from the past or a set of sexist tropes that we resist. Singers and program notes in the concert hall more often than not apologize for the piece as if it were a manifesto rather than a work of art from long ago.

It is true that the apparent submissiveness of the poems

can be troubling. "Since I first saw him, I believe myself blind"; "You may not notice me, a lowly maiden"; "How could he from among all of them have uplifted and favoured lowly me"; "I shall serve him, live for him, belong wholly to him"; "Let me in humility bow down to my lord."

Two musicologists—Kristina Muxfeldt in her influential article *"Frauenliebe und Leben*: Now and Then,"[11] and Rufus Hallmark in his book-length study *"Frauenliebe und Leben":* *Chamisso's Poems and Schumann's Songs*[12]—have attempted to contextualize and to some extent rescue the program of Schumann's cycle and the poetry of Adelbert von Chamisso that it sets.

Little known now except as the author of *Frauenliebe*, Chamisso was not a sentimental hack but a self-consciously progressive poet whose reputation stretched into the twentieth century and merited an admiring essay by Thomas Mann. Chamisso wrote a great deal of verse in a female voice, and his avowed aim was not so much to impose or reinforce a regressive patriarchal ideology as to make space for a female perspective in a poetic economy starved of female experience. Furthermore, Chamisso did, as an editor, publish poetry by women. However, the perceived need to ventriloquize the female voice in a cycle like *Frauenliebe* is not a comfortable one for modern audiences. Nevertheless many of the tropes of *Frauenliebe* are borrowed from the catalog not of female but of male submission in love, something Schumann surely acknowledges in a song like the second one of the cycle, "Er der herrlichste von allen," with its fanfare-like motif in voice and piano, traditional chivalric rhetoric transferred to the female voice. The sheer passion of *Frauenliebe*'s rhetoric, musically and poetically, is a world away from the nineteenth-century ideal of the sexless, passive angel in the house.

So what we confront in singing and playing and hearing *Frauenliebe* today is a necessary complexity, the complexity of confronting a passionate woman brought to life in words and music by two mid-nineteenth-century men and, in turn, usually impersonated by a twenty-first-century female singer.[13] The overarching theme of the cycle is, surely, not submission but loss—this is the final effect of the expressive arc of the cycle, the key to its emotional power, its visceral and aesthetic impact, as analyzed with technical bravura by Charles Rosen. Nevertheless, it's worth remembering the discomfited response of even nineteenth-century listeners to the submissive side of *Frauenliebe*. Theodor Storm wrote to his fellow writer Paul Heyse in 1874, "Mörike [the poet] once told me how distasteful all this was to him, and these are exactly my sentiments."[14]

Looking at how Schumann's *Frauenliebe* came into being can, however, deepen our response to it and further elaborate the tensions of identity that give it life. It was Gustave Flaubert who famously declared, "I am Madame Bovary," and in many senses it is Robert Schumann himself who is the protagonist of *Frauenliebe und Leben*.[15]

Schumann wrote the *Frauenliebe und Leben* cycle in the magical year of 1840, the year in which he wrote almost all of his famous song cycles—*Dichterliebe*, the op. 24 and op. 39 *Liederkreisen*, to poems by Heine and Eichendorff, respectively, and the Kerner Lieder op. 35. One of the cycles, *Myrthen*, was explicitly intended as a wedding gift, a garland of myrtles to celebrate his impending union with the famous pianist and active composer Clara Wieck. Robert had met Clara when he had lodged with her family as a piano student of her father, the legendary teacher Friedrich Wieck. Friedrich had raised Clara to be a great virtuoso, and he resisted her marriage to Schumann to the bitter end.

The 1840 flowering of song, a genre that Schumann, the master of the piano miniature, had hitherto avoided, spoke to that sense of elated productivity that stemmed in turn from the coming to fruition of the struggle to marry Clara. In true Romantic vein, and reflecting the legal and personal struggles surrounding their union, these cycles are full of love, jealousy, rejection, fury, frustration—all the feelings that had surged and struggled in Schumann's head since he first committed himself to Clara. As the conflict reached its apogee in 1839/1840, Robert was almost overwhelmed.

Frauenliebe emerged from this maelstrom in July 1840. June had been a month of intense legal argument, and the marriage was to be finally celebrated in September. It reflects the singular but vexed closeness that bound together these two extraordinary musicians—Robert, the creator of new forms in music, and Clara, one of the greatest pianists of her day and a composer too. If anything is likely to confirm that *Frauenliebe* is not a straightforwardly soupy celebration of female subjection, it is that it was written by Robert with Clara in mind. Clara was a potentially brilliant composer (the current revival of her early piano concerto is leading to a reassessment of this lost talent—she largely gave up composing not long into her marriage), and she was one of the star pianists of the day, a much bigger name than Schumann. Schumann's attitude towards his fiancée remained highly conflicted.

His admiration for her as an artist was profound and lasting—"My Clara played everything like a master," he could declare in the second year of their marriage[16]—but at the same time it was compromised by a desire for her to give herself to him as a wife and not an artist. A letter of September 1838 could move within a few lines from a declaration that her art was "great and holy" to an insistence that "my Clara will be a happy wife, a contented, beloved wife." A year later he was musing "about our first summer in Zwickau as married folks ... young wives must be able to cook and keep house if they want satisfied husbands." A few weeks later: "You *shall* forget the artist, you *shall* live only for yourself and your house and your husband." In the same year, Robert had asked Clara to "trust and obey me: after all, men are above women."[17]

The reality of the Schumanns' marriage was a complex one, recorded in depth in their marriage diaries, continually reflecting the pull between bourgeois convention and the life of the artist.[18] Clara did cease composing, but she continued her career as an internationally feted (and well-paid) pianist, often to her husband's frustration despite his admiration for her superlative artistry. *Frauenliebe* seems to encode Robert's desires and anxieties as much as it speaks for the role of the woman who was to become his wife so soon after its composition. Here he is in December 1838, prostrate before her, abject, submissive: "It is from you that I receive all life, on whom I am wholly dependent. Like a slave, I should often like to follow you from afar at a distance, and await your slightest bidding."[19]

Reading another passage from a letter from Robert to Clara of 1838, two years before their marriage, it is difficult not to think of one of the most famous songs of the *Frauenliebe* cycle, "Du Ring an meinem Finger," in which the bride apostrophizes her wedding ring and sings affectingly of her love for her husband. Here is the opening of the poem:

You ring on my finger,
My golden little ring,
I press you devoutly to my lips,
To my heart.

And here is Robert's troubled letter:

And now, since you value my ring so little, I care no longer for yours, since yesterday, and wear it no longer. I dreamed that I was walking by deep water—and an impulse seized me and I threw the ring into the water—and then I was filled with a passionate longing to plunge in after it.[20]

The deep identification that Robert felt between himself and Clara as their marriage approached is apparent in the envoi to a letter of March 1839 in which he muddles genders and blurs identities: "Adieu my heart of hearts, beloved brother of my heart, dearest husband [the masculine form of spouse, *Ehegemahl*], adieu, I love you with all my heart." He signs the letter not as Robert Schumann but as Robert Wieck.[21]

So here are more layers of complexity to add to our response to *Frauenliebe* and to the construction of the identity of its protagonist-persona: Schumann's own anxieties and ambivalences about his relationship with Clara and his own deep identification with her.

What then would it mean for a man to sing *Frauenliebe*? There is a long tradition of lieder in a male voice being sung by women, from Schubert's own day to our own. *Frauenliebe* is today largely a female preserve, despite the recent intervention of some distinguished male voices such as the baritones Matthias Goerne and Roderick Williams.[22] It is fascinating to note, however, that probably the earliest concert performance of the whole cycle, with Clara Schumann herself at the piano, was given by a man, the baritone Julius Stockhausen, in 1862.[23] Our complex relationship to this masterpiece, our recognition of its compositional and performative strata, layer on layer, should loosen the straitjacket of gender-normative performance and allow us to react to the full range of the possible worlds it creates. I hope to find an opportunity to perform *Frauenliebe* in the future. It belongs to us all; all performers can find in it an expression of universal human concerns and experiences, subtle and multivalent articulations of subjectivity and emotional engagement. Even in the most apparently gendered of pieces, gender remains complex and fluid, and our responses as performers and spectators or listeners are open and nonbinary.

⊢

Confusions of identity have been long-standing features of the carnival in Christian culture, and the carnivalesque has gone on to be a recurring feature of opera from its origins through to the present day. Gender confusion of all sorts has been as much a feature of opera as of Shakespearean comedy, and in far more overt, if sometimes less tangled, forms than in *Combattimento*. The best-known examples in the canonical repertoire of today involve female-to-male cross-dressing. Cherubino, the pubescent boy of Mozart's *Marriage of Figaro*, is played by a mezzo-soprano, with a Shakespearean touch when this feigning boy feigns to be a girl in order to avoid being sent away to join the army. In Strauss and Hoffmanstahl's decadent and titillating Mozartian homage *Der Rosenkavalier*, the opera opens with two female singers in bed together, a soprano and a mezzo-soprano, playing a woman and a man: respectively Princess Marie Thérèse von Werdenberg (the Marschallin) and her teenage lover, Octavian, the Count Rofrano, who impersonates a maid, Mariandel, in order to bamboozle and eventually humiliate the oafish Baron Ochs.

The era of the operatic castrato—stretching from Monteverdi right through to the early nineteenth century—had earlier provided all sorts of opportunities for gender confusion (castrated men with high voices singing both female and male parts) and, in the eighteenth century, opera seria enthroned a counterintuitive ideal in which the heroic male—Julius Caesar say, or Alexander the Great—was almost always played by a thrillingly and prodigiously voiced eunuch, with the power of a man but with the high pitch of a woman. Challenges to normative notions of gender in the licensed space of the opera house continued into the later twentieth century. Yet the work I am going to look at now, Benjamin Britten's *Curlew River*, is remarkable for the way in which, far from adopting a pose of titillation or subversion, it uses gender reversal to produce, both musically and dramatically, an abstract, supragendered portrayal of universal humanity transfigured.

Curlew River was the first of what Britten called his "parables for church performance." The central role in the piece, the Madwoman, is played by a male-voiced singer. It was written for the composer's partner, the tenor Peter Pears, in the first production in 1964. I want to explore what the casting of a man in the role of a mother means for the piece and for our response to it.

The first of three such works, *Curlew River* was inspired by Britten's encounter with the Japanese Noh play *Sumidagawa*. Stylized in movement, with the traditionally all-male cast, *Sumidagawa* tells the story of a noblewoman who has been driven mad by the loss of her only son. She comes to the banks of the Sumida River, and while crossing it hears a story told by the ferryman, who had been mockingly reluctant to take her as a passenger. It becomes clear that the woman's son had been kidnapped by a slave trader and, sickeningly, left to die by his captor alongside the river precisely a year ago. The villagers are even now commemorating the hideous event in prayer. The mother herself prays, and the ghost of the boy appears to her; but

FIGURE 1. Tsukioka Kôgyo, *Sumidagawa*, from the series *Pictures of Nō Performances (Nogaku Zue)*, 1893–1903. Color woodblock print. Art Institute of Chicago, Frederick W. Gookin Collection.

As she seeks to grasp it by the hand,
The shape begins to fade away;
The vision fades and reappears
And stronger grows her yearning.[24]

Britten, on tour in Japan with Pears in February 1956, was taken to a performance of *Sumidagawa*:

> The whole occasion made a tremendous impression upon me: the simple, touching story, the economy of style, the intense slowness of the action, the marvellous skill and control of the performers, the beautiful costumes, the mixture of chanting, speech, singing which, with the three instruments, made up the strange music—it all offered a totally new "operatic" experience.

There was no conductor—the instrumentalists sat on the stage, as did the chorus, and the chief characters made their entrance down a long ramp. The lighting was strictly non-theatrical. The cast was all male, the one female character wearing an exquisite mask made no attempt to hide the male jowl beneath it.[25]

Seized by the power of *Sumidagawa*, Britten and his collaborator librettist William Plomer created a Christianized version, almost identical in its plotline and preserving many lines of dialogue apart from one crucial change. Noh plays typically had a happy ending, which the fifteenth-century author of *Sumidagawa*, Jūrō Motomasa, had subverted with a tragic moment of loss. In Britten and Plomer's Christian reworking, the appearance of the spirit of the Madwoman's kidnapped son at the climax of the piece, despite the tragedy of his death, effects a consolation that allows her to join in a communal amen.

Go your way in peace, mother,

the boy sings,

The dead shall rise again
And in that blessed day
We shall meet in heaven.
God be with you all.
God be with you, mother.

God's grace cures the Madwoman of her madness. Atonement is achieved.

The genesis of *Curlew River* reflects not only the happenstance of Britten's trip to Japan and experience of *Sumidagawa* (at the behest, it should be said, of William Plomer, who had spent some years in Japan in the 1920s) but also his interest in the theatrical experiments of the first half of the twentieth century. The Noh tradition was first co-opted into modernism by W. B. Yeats and Ezra Pound (close friends in the years before and during the First World War): Pound translated Noh plays, and both poets wrote plays in the Noh style. The young Britten himself, indeed, was marginally involved in one of these Noh projects, helping to find a gong player for Pound's recitation of one of his translations for the Mercury Theatre in 1938.

An early piece of Noh-derived music theater in the Western tradition was Bertolt Brecht and Kurt Weill's *Der Jasager* (1930), a *Schuloper* or *Lehrstück*, based on Arthur Waley's translation of the fifteenth-century Noh play *Taniko*, roughly contemporaneous with *Sumidagawa*. A boy, hoping to obtain medicine for his sick mother, travels over a dangerous mountain pass with a group of students; falling ill himself, he sacrifices himself to the common good and allows himself to be flung into the abyss.

Der Jasager has none of the populist qualities of the Brecht/Weill hit masterpiece of 1928, *The Threepenny Opera*, but both pieces spring from the same interest in a didactic theater. Both were staging posts on the way towards Brecht's fully developed ideas of epic theater and the so-called *Verfremdungseffekt*: the alienation or distancing effect in which both audience and actors are prevented from losing themselves completely in the narrative. The ideal is rather that of the conscious and critical observer. Classic Brechtian devices to achieve this include direct address to the audience, interruption of the narrative, and, more generally, drawing attention to the theatrical process itself, in direct contrast to the fourth-wall orthodoxy of the nineteenth-century theater, in which the audience is supposed to imagine itself eavesdropping on reality. At first sight *Der Jasager*, an unforgiving exercise in music theater as agitprop, might seem a million miles away from *Curlew River*. And Britten's theatrical affinities were more in the Movement Theatre of the 1930s and the French tradition that underlay his much earlier opera, *The Rape of Lucretia*, based on a play in French by André Obey. Britten was unimpressed by the *Threepenny Opera*, and *Der Jasager* was not seen in the UK until after *Curlew River*. Yet many features of Britten's work echo the preoccupations that produced *Der Jasager*. The political message, the political aim, and the structure may have been rendered religious, but many of the theatrical aims remain the same: demolition of the fourth wall, narrative interruption, a focus on theatrical process.

Whatever Britten's own religious leanings or beliefs, he did repeatedly return to the use of religious rituals, practices, and formulas as a framing device in his work. In the chamber opera *The Rape of Lucretia* (1947), for instance, the male and female choruses, Christian figures from an unspecified future, comment on the pagan action that takes center stage; but they are also drawn into the action, visibly and disconcertingly blurring the lines between narration, commentary, and action.

But it was medieval religious ritual that again and again supplied the framing devices for Britten's vocal works, both the overtly theatrical and pieces that are, in one way or another, dramatic.[26] Take an early masterpiece like the Christmas favorite, the *Ceremony of Carols*—settings of fourteenth- and fifteenth-century texts for boys choir and harp—that

Britten turned into a ritual by enclosing it within processional and recessional chants in unison based on the Gregorian antiphon "Hodie Christus natus est" and in its significant naming as a "Ceremony." Medievalism is also on display obliquely in the piece for two voices and piano, *Canticle Two: Abraham and Isaac*, based on a medieval mystery play, and in its most developed form to that date in *Noye's Fludde*, an opera for amateurs and children, based on a text from the same Chester cycle as canticle 2.

Britten's coup with *Curlew River*—a coup that his librettist Plomer fully recognized—was the decision to refract *Sumidagawa* through the lens of medieval Christianity. This avoided all Britten's long-nurtured worries about fake exoticism and superficial Japonisme, preserving within a European setting all the performative aspects of the Noh original that made such an appeal to the modernist theatrical aesthetic. Instead of slavishly mimicking Noh music, Britten used a small instrumental group, inspired by the Noh ensemble, to create a unique but equally austere soundworld, melding together typically Western and typically Eastern musical practices, timbres, and harmonic devices. It doesn't sound like pastiche but like a new and autonomous development in Britten's quest for an authentic musical language.

A group of monks processes into the performance space, a church, singing the medieval plainchant "Te lucis ante terminum"; the presiding abbot announces that the community will enact a story of how a woman was saved by God's grace. The theatrical frame of the monastic community is paralleled and reinforced in the musical sphere by the use of plainchant. "Te lucis" is the source, Britten tells us, "from which the whole piece may be said to have grown."[27] And the redemptive climax is musically achieved by another plainchant hymn, "Custodes hominum." The monks who are to play the three principal roles—the Madwoman, the Traveller, and the Ferryman—are "ceremonially prepared," donning costumes and half masks (in the Noh play only one character, the Madwoman, is fully masked). *Curlew River* is, then, a very particular instantiation of that multifaceted twentieth-century reinvention of the theatrical—antirealist in its thrust and moral in its intention—presenting us with an exemplum of Auden's parable art—"that art which shall teach man to unlearn hatred and learn love"—to match Brecht's own parable drama from the East, *The Good Person of Szechuan.*[28]

Returning, then, to the issue of gender and identity, how crucial is the Madwoman's femininity or femaleness to Curlew River? It is obviously a feature of the theatrical conventions that Britten inherited from Noh theater and transformed into a Christian mystery play.

It's easy to be confused by the whole business of sexual ambiguity in Britten's output, reinforced as it is by the critical tradition of focusing on sexuality in writing about pieces like *Les illuminations* (his sensuous and excitable setting of Rimbaud for string orchestra), *The Turn of the Screw* (bathed, like the James story on which it is based, in a murky half light of sinister implication), and *Death in Venice* (so often misconceived as a pederastic hymn cum swan song). Humphrey Carpenter, Britten's first biographer, writes that in *Curlew River*, "the casting of a male singer was, of course, suggested by the Noh play, but like the use of a countertenor as Oberon [in Britten's 1960 Shakespearean opera, *A Midsummer Night's Dream*] it carries hints of unorthodox sexuality."[29] This is quite wrong. The casting of a male singer was not, of course, "suggested" but actually a cardinal feature inherited from the Noh original; and the playing of the Madwoman by a man has nothing

FIGURE 2. Peter Pears in *Curlew River*, 1964. Reg Wilson/Shutterstock.

to do with "unorthodox sexuality." Carpenter was writing at
a time when, understandably, in the wake of Philip Brett's re-
velatory writing,[30] explorations of the sexual currents flowing
through Britten's work were prominent.

Britten's friends were concerned by Pears's casting as the
Madwoman, worrying that the effect might be like that of a
pantomime dame, something teetering into the ridiculous,
and there was a precedent for this in Britten's writing for
Pears. Only three years before *Curlew River*, comical cross-
gender casting, inherited from Shakespeare, enlivened the
sorry tale of the tragical lovers Pyramus and Thisbe in the
aforementioned opera *A Midsummer Night's Dream*. The composer uses the faltering falsetto of Francis Flute, the bellows
mender—played by Peter Pears—to tragicomic effect in his
ludicrous performance of Thisbe. Looking at the photographs
of the first production, one can easily see that the comedy
of Pear's performance was grounded in a play with the ste-
reotypes of comic female impersonation. The send-up of the
reigning bel canto diva, Joan Sutherland, was widely recognized. The music underlines Sutherland's ghostly presence,
with its echoes of Donizetti's heroines and use of the flute as
an indicator of mental distraction. That the defining instrumental timbre of the Noh ensemble is the flute is a suggestive
coincidence.

But the Madwoman in *Curlew River* is not a female impersonator, and there is nothing funny or sexually unorthodox about her. Sexuality is absent. Britten's fascination with
Sumidagawa was above all a response to its "solemn dedication," and he noted that "the one female character wearing
an exquisite mask made no attempt to hide the male jowl beneath it." Noh theater, from which *Curlew River* flowed, is not
Kabuki, the Japanese theatrical form perhaps most famous in

FIGURE 3. Production photograph of Benjamin Britten's opera *A Midsummer Night's Dream*, act 3, the Rustics' Play, from the Holland Festival, July 1960. From left, the Wall/Snout (Edward Byles) offering a chink to Thisbe/Flute (Peter Pears), who is addressing it. The two cast members seated on the right are Helena (Joan Carlyle) and Demetrius (Thomas Hemsley). Photograph by Maria Austria, 1960, © Maria Austria Instituut. Image provided by Britten Pears Arts (brittenpearsarts .org). Ref: PHPH/10/1/27.

the West for its central female impersonator, the Onnagata. Kabuki and Noh are both highly stylized, but where Noh is austere and still, slow and economical, Kabuki is glamorous and exaggerated. While Britten was excited by his experience of Kabuki on that same 1956 trip that introduced him to Noh, he didn't use Kabuki influences until the third of his parables, *The Burning Fiery Furnace*, with its self-conscious theatrical contrast between the extravagant and the austere.

A Kabuki version of *Sumidagawa* was presented in 1919, and it is here that the crosscurrents from West to East and East to West begin to become a little dizzying. Pound's version of

Noh style was partly devised by a Japanese dancer, Michio Ito, who had studied with Dalcroze, the inventor of eurhythmics; Diaghilev had his dancers prepared for the *Rite of Spring* by attending Dalcroze classes. The Kabuki *Sumidagawa* in 1919 was inspired by Diaghilev's Russian ballets seen by the Kabuki actor Ichikawa Ennosuke II during his European study tour. Britten's movement coach for Curlew River was Claude Chagrin, trained in the French mime school, which had itself been influenced by Japanese performance styles.

The aesthetic that informs the creation of an idealized, essentialized, and exotic form of female identity in Kabuki has little or nothing to do with the Madwoman in either *Sumidagawa* or Britten's church parable. "Onnagata became highly skilled at producing a high-pitched falsetto for many hours a day, all their lives," writes one Kabuki commentator, Ronald Cavaye: "over many years and with countless subtle alterations and refinements of technique, the Onnagata developed a characterisation that, while highly stylised, is convincing enough to be recognisable as a *real woman*."[31] While more recent commentators have emphasized the stylization of the Onnagata performance, contesting the idea of essential femininity and emphasizing the paradoxical influence of Onnagata styles on standards of feminine beauty more widely, it remains the case that sensuality and sexuality were at the core of the Onnagata practice.

Noh theater is far away from all this. In *Curlew River*, the playing of a grieving mother by an unmistakably male-voiced singer, masked, is part of Britten's participation in the desire of practitioners in the twentieth century to enhance the performativity of theater, to move away from realism and embrace more generally the doctrines of formalism and a sort of emotional detachment, a making strange. The roots of these trends lie deep in twentieth-century musical and theatrical culture, and they twist and diverge endlessly, much to our confusion. But if the impact of the First World War was to entrench a sort of emotional reticence, which went together with a condemnation of the sentimentalism of much Romantic art, then the disappearance of silent cinema and the advent of the compelling realism of the talkies were to put pressure on live performance to be more performative, more strange, less real.

In playing the piece in the anniversary year of Britten's birth, 2013, some fifty years after the premiere of *Curlew River*, we went maskless and gestureless, Noh theater–less as it were. The performance took place as part of the London Barbican's Britten celebrations and was staged in St. Giles Cripplegate, a medieval church embedded in the Barbican's brutalist modernism and surrounded by water. The production, by the director Netia Jones, made extensive use of video. I played the Madwoman as I would have done any other part in classical music theater, shifting gears between the formal and the informal, the detached and the engaged, the realistic, the expressionistic, and the ritualistic. This is the postmodern way in classical music theater, a healthy and omnivorous eclecticism, wary of any one dominating theory while inheriting the theories of the past.

As part of that process of eclectic engagement with the piece, we did not emphasize the question of gender in the production, but let it, as it were, float. In the end, this is not a lead tenor role that fits into the hypermasculine inheritance of the operatic mainstream; but neither, as I played it, did questions of the play of gender impersonation cross my mind or inflect my voice or my movements. My costume was quite deliberately ungendered, neither male nor female. Having a tenor play the Madwoman, without all the Noh apparatus, retains the crucial element of distancing while at the same time broadening the appeal at the emotional core of the piece: this is a mother, a parent, a woman, a human being. One only has to imagine how different the piece would have been had Britten written it as a vehicle for a soprano rather than a tenor. This is storytelling, in the end, and as such, all efforts to restrain and contain emotion—like the casting of a man in the role of the mother—are a means ultimately and paradoxically to amplify the force of the story and carry the audience with us. Gender is blurred and, ultimately, transcended.

I studied Brecht's play *The Life of Galileo* as a teenage student of German, and at that time, in the 1980s, at the National Theatre in London, I saw a performance of the role by a great stage actor, Michael Gambon. Ultimately Galileo, despite all Brecht's protestations to the contrary, moves us, working through and beyond Brecht's theories about epic theater. *Curlew River* is the same sort of piece, and its origins in twentieth-century experiments and Japanese influences melt into the background as, like all the best works of art, it is set free from the circumstances of its origin, and from its creator and his preoccupations, to find its own life. The Madwoman in *Curlew River* is all of us (plate 2).

PLATE 1. Domenico Tintoretto, *Tancred Baptizing Clorinda*, 1586–1600. Oil on canvas; 66 ⁵/₁₆ × 45 ³/₁₆ in. (168.4 × 114.8 cm). The Museum of Fine Arts, Houston, The Samuel H. Kress Collection, 61.77. Photograph © The Museum of Fine Arts, Houston; Jud Haggard, photographer.

PLATE 2. "Is it you, my child?" Production photograph of US premiere of Benjamin Britten's *Curlew River*, from the Synod House, Cathedral of St. John the Divine, New York City, October 26, 2014, featuring Ian Bostridge as Madwoman. Photograph © Richard Termine, 2014.

PLATE 3. Anthony van Dyck, *Thomas Howard Count of Arundel and His Wife Alathea Talbot*, 1639–1640. Oil on canvas. Courtesy of Kunsthistorisches Museum Wien, Gemäldegalerie.

PLATE 4. "No doubt the signore will be leaving us soon. We must all lose what we thought to enjoy the best." Production photograph of Benjamin Britten's *Death in Venice*, London Coliseum, May 2007. Pictured left to right: Peter van Hulle (Hotel Porter), Peter Coleman Wright (Hotel Manager), Ian Bostridge (Aschenbach). Clive Barda / ArenaPAL.

2
Hidden
Histories

Ventriloquism and Identity in
Ravel's Chansons madécasses

There is no document of civilisation which is not at the same
time a document of barbarism.

WALTER BENJAMIN, "Theses on the Philosophy of History VII"

As a singer, my practice has inescapably involved questions
of identity and performativity, in the roles I have played
on the stage and, indeed, in singing chamber works such as
the lieder of Schubert or Schumann. When you perform as a
singer you take on a voice, but to what extent is that voice
your own? Or the composer's? Or that of the poet or librettist? And to what extent does the piece of music you perform
bring with it a silent, sometimes unacknowledged, history
that might pose questions that are rarely acknowledged in
the concert hall?

As Antonio Gramsci famously put it in his *Prison Notebooks*, "The starting point of critical elaboration is to have a
consciousness of what one really is, with self-knowledge as
a product of a historical process that has deposited up until
now an infinity of traces, without the benefit of an inventory."[1]

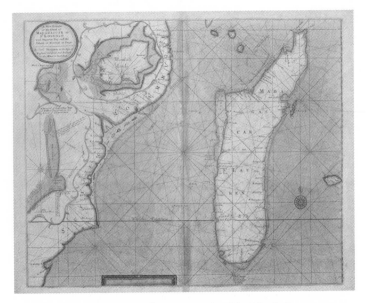

FIGURE 4. Samuel Thornton, "A New Draught of the Island of MADAGASCAR ats St. LORENZO with Augustin Bay and the Island of Mombass at Large," from *The Sea-Atlas: Containing an Hydrographical Description of most of the Sea-Coasts of the Known Parts of the World* (1702–1707). Lionel Pincus and Princess Firyal Map Division, The New York Public Library. Courtesy of The New York Public Library Digital Collections, https://digitalcollections.nypl.org/items/510d47e4 -65cb-a3d9-e040-e00a18064a99.

This is the point of my excavations here—looking at different facets of pieces of classical music, undertaking a critical elaboration, and building an inventory.

Written in 1925 and 1926, Maurice Ravel's *Chansons madécasses* (Songs of Madagascar or Malagasy Songs) has become a canonical feature of the classical repertoire. The cycle consists of three songs scored for the unusual combination of voice, cello, flute, and piano. Technically demanding for the singer, it is often performed in concert and has been recorded many times, starting with the 1931 recording by Ravel himself with the mezzo-soprano Madeleine Grey. Some of the greatest singers of the twentieth century—Dietrich Fischer-Dieskau, Jessye Norman, Janet Baker, Gérard Souzay—performed and recorded it.

Yet over the last century, the attitude to the piece in concert programs, record sleeves, and CD booklets has been almost entirely an aesthetic one that doesn't engage with the ambivalent texture or extraordinary origins of the piece. Recent movements towards interrogating, broadening, and decolonizing the canon are relevant here. Decolonizing is not only a matter of bringing new and previously unheard music into the canon. It's also a matter of interrogating works within the preexisting canon, building that inventory Gramsci talks about.

These songs of Ravel's were composed by a Parisian who never visited Madagascar about what can only have been an imagined Madagascar as far as he was concerned. Surely we need to ask, as performers, what is the history of the relationship between France and Madagascar rather than simply accepting Madagascar as an abstract and exotic location, a fairy tale? As I shall show, what's hidden beneath the surface is a highly complex political geography, a story of power relations, violence, and European attitudes to the perceived "other."

The texts of the three songs that make up the *Chansons madécasses* are taken from a longer work of prose poems by the late eighteenth-century writer Evariste Parny, all written in the ventriloquized voices of the indigenous inhabitants of the island. As we shall see, unlike Maurice Ravel, Evariste Parny had a close personal and historical connection to the island of Madagascar, which had faced, at the time Parny was writing, a succession of attempts at colonization by European powers. It was only in the 1890s that the island succumbed to French conquest. Madagascar was and is unique: as the fourth largest island in the world, with an ecologically distinct flora and fauna; as a nexus of cultural influences and populations—Austronesian, Arab, East African; and as a matrix of highly complex and differentiated social and political systems. It was, nevertheless, in the end, swallowed whole by the French state as one of the last acts of the so-called scramble for Africa. By the time Ravel composed his songs to Parny's texts, the meaning of Madagascar had changed in the French imagination. The colonial projects of the seventeenth and eighteenth centuries differed vastly from those of the age of imperialism around 1900. And by the 1920s, colonialism had become a site of political controversy between the left and right in France itself. *Chansons madécasses* was written at a febrile moment in French colonial history, and at its first performance it was in fact greeted as a provocative political statement, something often forgotten in concert performances today.

The *Chansons madécasses* are often described as beautiful and exotic, with that notion of the exotic—to redeploy Gramsci—"uninventoried" in terms of its history in relation to European fantasies of non-European cultures. As I've said, the piece consists of three songs. The first and third indeed deploy some of the exoticizing gestures that Ravel had previously used—and to some degree satirized by overinflation—in his famous orchestral song cycle *Shéhérazade*, inspired by the world of the *Arabian Nights*. That text's popularity in Europe encoded the undifferentiated "othering" of non-European cultures. The musical motifs orientalism engendered in European classical music were divorced from the actual musical practices of those cultures yet were defined in the West by fetishized inflections of the Western harmonic tradition, definitively explored in the work of the musicologist Ralph

Locke.[2] It's a huge and complex field. Suffice it to say that in the first and third songs of the *madécasses* cycle, Ravel with breathtaking originality blends together a soundworld clearly influenced by the early twentieth-century vogue for non-European textures with an overall *Affekt* that remains exoticizing in its lazy sensuality and intense eroticism.

But the second song of the *madécasses* cycle, with which I shall be concerned here, is very different. Harsh and hard-hitting, it uses its bare scoring to reject the sensual bath of standard exoticizing musical tropes.

The words and sounds of the song are here very far from offering a comfortable fantasy to European listeners. Spoken in the imagined voice of a Malagasy, the text begins "Méfiez vous des blancs" (Beware of the white people), and it ends by announcing that European invaders are not welcome in Madagascar and stating that they have been roundly repelled.

The text is an anticolonialist cry of liberty, though it is a complex one: written not by a Malagasy but by a French colonial born on the nearby Île Bourbon (now Réunion) and brought up by enslaved people, largely of Malagasy origin, working as domestic servants—a man whose fortune was founded on a commodity economy worked on by enslaved people traded (mostly) from Madagascar.

So, where did this cry come from in 1787, and what could it have meant when Ravel created his setting in the mid-1920s? I want to start by taking a look at Madagascar, at failed French attempts to colonize it, and at the poet Evariste Parny's relationship to Madagascar and its people.

Situated four hundred kilometers off the east coast of southern Africa, Madagascar is a vast island, 1,600 kilometers long and up to 570 kilometers wide. Ecologically isolated for tens of millions of years, it was first settled by voyagers from

East Asia as early as the fifth century BCE. It subsequently became a crucible for a complex interaction between African, Arabic, and Austronesian cultures. By the seventeenth century it already had a long history of trade with both the African mainland and the Arabian peninsula, especially in enslaved people, captured during raids on each other by the different kingdoms into which the island's population segmented. However, it was the opening up of European markets in that period that allowed the various kingdoms of Madagascar to consolidate their wealth and power. As a recent historian puts it,

> During the seventeenth century monarchies with quite extensive control were to emerge in several areas of the island, particularly in places where kings were able to combine a higher ideology of monarchy with an enhanced commercial role that was partly the result of the growth in trade with Europeans. The rise of the powerful kingdoms makes the seventeenth century a turning-point in Madagascar's history.[3]

The island of Madagascar was the object of European desire and the subject of European fantasy from the very outset of the European colonial enterprise in the late fifteenth century, starting with the Portuguese. It was coveted as both a staging post on the way to the East Indies and a possible site for a lucrative settlement. The English were certainly keen. Sir Thomas Herbert in 1658 called Madagascar the "Empress among Islands," while Admiral Sir William Monson in 1650 had imagined it becoming a rival to the English plantation in Virginia. Prince Rupert of the Rhine had a scheme in mind in the 1630s for conquering the island, which his mother, the exiled Queen of Bohemia, fondly described as his "Romance of Madagascar . . . like one of Don Quixote's conquests."[4] Another English scheme is commemorated in the portrait of the Earl and Countess of Arundel by van Dyck, gesturing towards a globe on which Madagascar has a central place (plate 3). None of the English plans got off the ground, but in the 1640s the French forged a plan to "take possession of the island, to dwell there, and to . . . trade."[5] Under the sponsorship of Cardinal Richelieu, the Société françoise de l'orient sent one Jacques Pronis in pursuit of this objective. En route, he succeeded in claiming one of the Mascarene islands, which he called Île Bourbon (now known as Réunion), the small island where, as we shall see, the poet of the *Chansons madécasses*, Parny, was born a century or so later. Pronis went on to build a settlement in the south of Madagascar that he called Fort Dauphin.

Pronis's project was riven by conflict among the settlers themselves—who were endlessly afflicted with fevers—and between the settlers and the indigenous Malagasy, who were especially enraged when Pronis treacherously sold some sixty-three friendly *indigènes* as enslaved people to the Dutch governor of nearby Mauritius. An attempted revolt against Pronis led him to exile a dozen or so of the mutineers to the Île Bourbon, an unpropitious beginning to the French settlement of that island. Back in Paris the shareholders of the Société became concerned and sent one of their number, Étienne de Flacourt, to sort things out, "to establish the glory of the French name and that of Christian piety,"[6] the religious motivation not an inconsiderable one in these efforts to subdue Madagascar.

Flacourt's mission at Fort Dauphin was a failure, distinguished for the intensity of the violence he rained down upon the population and for the ultimately successful resistance of the inhabitants despite the superiority of French weaponry. In two years Flacourt and his men pillaged and burned over fifty villages, but the experience of the French settlers was hunger, fever, and endless conflict. For the Société back in Paris, returns were paltry, the prospect of future returns ever receding. The settlement was eventually ignominiously abandoned by the French in 1674. One lasting result was that Flacourt penned two important books of history and natural history about the island. He also, as we shall see, left an inscribed marble monument as a record of his misadventures and as a warning to others.[7]

Despite this disaster, French fascination with the great isle of Madagascar continued through the seventeenth century and into the eighteenth, in more or less fantastical forms. Trade continued with the island's kingdoms, and so did visionary schemes of conquest or settlement.

Between 1768 and 1771, a correspondent of Voltaire, the Comte de Maudave, launched a vauntedly enlightened colonial venture that aimed to cooperate with the Malagasy people and suppress the slave trade. It ended in tensions between French and Malagasy, money problems, fever, and the hypocritical spectacle of Maudave siphoning off a hundred enslaved people to man his own plantations on the Île de France (Mauritius), the adjoining island to the Île Bourbon.

Further schemes to conquer Madagascar by the Munchausenesque self-styled "baron" de Benyovski, a fantasy-spinning Polish Hungarian adventurer, started with French support in 1773, support that was withdrawn as the old story of fever and conflict with the locals predictably ended any prospect of a successful colony. Two government inspectors concluded that it would be best "to give up all idea of founding a colony on an island which, at all times, had been the grave of so many Frenchmen." The trading post was shut in 1779, and when Benyovski tried to revive his venture in 1784 as "European plenipotentiary" for Madagascar—with the supposed support of the Emperor of Austria and two Baltimore slave traders—French troops arrived to put a stop to the chaos. They ambushed and shot dead the unfortunate count in May 1786, just a year before the publication of Evariste Parny's *Chansons madécasses* and its powerful evocation of the inhabitants' resistance to European incursion: "Méfiez vous des blancs" (Beware of the whites). The island of Madagascar remained resolutely uncolonized until the very end of the nineteenth century.[8]

—

Many of the French would-be colonists from the failed Fort Dauphin settlement on Madagascar—evacuated in 1674— went on to settle on the Île Bourbon, one of the Mascarene islands, 800 kilometers from Madagascar. By the beginning of the eighteenth century, it still had only 1,100 inhabitants and remained largely undeveloped.

An influx of retired pirates changed all this (piracy was endemic in the area). They constituted as much as 48 percent of the population by 1710. Many were wealthy and started bringing enslaved people from Madagascar and East Africa to Île Bourbon, where they cleared the land for agriculture. The French East India Company revived its interest, transplanting coffee plants and achieving up to two and a half million pounds production annually by the mid-1700s. "Nothing is more beautiful," Governor Dumas declared to the directors of the company in 1728, "than the coffee plantations stretching out to infinity." Slavery was formally licensed in 1723 in an Indian Ocean version of the West Indian "Code Noir."[9]

The population of the island grew by leaps and bounds, reaching twenty thousand by 1764. As the economist Thomas Piketty has recently underlined in his massive study, *Capital and Ideology*, the French social system adopted on an island like the Île Bourbon was uniquely tilted towards slavery and the economics of commodity production for the international market. The Indian Ocean slave trade predated European engagement in the area, but the capitalist dynamics of the eighteenth century drove it to a level of unprecedented intensity. There was a historically unparalleled proportion of enslaved people in the population of the Île Bourbon: 80 percent, or 15,800 enslaved versus 4,200 free men in 1764 when Evariste Parny, the author of the *Chansons madécasses*, was eleven years old. The largest concentration of enslaved people in the Euro-American world on the eve of the French Revolution of 1789 was on French island colonies, east and west. By the 1780s they numbered in total some one hundred thousand.[10]

Settlers made their way to the Île Bourbon to make their fortune. One notary estimated the return on capital as 10 percent per annum in 1756 compared to a paltry 5 percent in metropolitan France. The governor sent to the island in 1727, Benoit Dumas, made fabulous gains, doubling his fortune in less than eight years.[11]

It was on this island, paradise and prison as he called it, that the poet of the *Chansons madécasses*, Evariste Parny, was born on February 6, 1753. His birth coincided with the beginning of a decline in the fortunes of the island caused by a fall in the price of coffee as French Caribbean and Dutch Javan beans began to enter the global marketplace. Land fragmentation due to French inheritance customs and a series of natural disasters—cyclones and a plague of aphids—only intensified the economic pressure.

The Parny family had been the beneficiaries of the swift rise in fortunes that the slave-dominated economy could offer at a time when naked commerce was driving the globalization of the day. Evariste's grandfather, Pierre Parny, a baker, arrived on the island in 1698 as part of the entourage of the new governor. He married Barbe, daughter of one François Mussard, a wealthy proprietor who was notorious as an escaped slave hunter. Pierre himself was adjudged "cruel to the point of barbarism towards his black slaves," his wife even more so. Their youngest son, Paul, Evariste's father, was born in 1717, educated in France, fought against the British in India, and died back on Bourbon, a lieutenant colonel and chevalier de Saint-Louis. His estates grew rice, wheat, corn, coffee, and cotton and were worked by enslaved people, a large proportion of whom came from Madagascar. Evariste, born on Bourbon, was educated in France, commissioned into the French army, traveled the world, and returned home in 1773 and 1783. He finally settled in France, where he died in 1814. The *Chansons madécasses* were written in Pondicherry (now Puducherry), French India, in 1785–1787, where he was serving as aide-de-camp to the governor general just after his final trip to the Île Bourbon.[12]

The assertive cry of liberty that Parny put into the mouth of an indigenous Malagasy is not straightforward in the context from which it emerged. Evariste Parny's own attitudes towards slavery and colonial settlement were complex and refracted through his upbringing on Bourbon; his travels as a young man to South America, India, and the Cape; and his long association with and residence in the metropolitan France of the Enlightenment, only a few years before the outbreak of the French Revolution. Writing (in verse) from Pondicherry in 1785 to his brother, he spoke blisteringly of "ce monde toujours désolé / Par l'Européen sanguinaire."[13] His instincts were anticolonial and antislavery while at the same time he remained deeply implicated, like so many other progressive voices, in a world dependent on colonial ventures and the slave trade: a colonial officer, after all, and a man who had inherited eighteen enslaved people from his mother when she died and stood to inherit yet more on the death of his father.

Evariste's mother had died when he was only five years old. He was educated initially by enslaved people of Malagasy origin working as domestic servants, absorbing, as Parny wrote to Bertin, "the tastes and manners"[14] of those with whom he lived. Tales of Madagascar were part of his childhood imaginarium, his bedtime stories, even if the bulk of his formal education was in metropolitan France. He remained fascinated by the Malagasy language.[15]

On his return visits to Bourbon in 1773 and 1783 he had liaisons with two enslaved women, Léda and Zette, both of Malagasy origin. The first of Parny's affairs with a Malagasy woman was not a casual encounter; it gave issue to a daughter, Valère, who took his name and was brought up by his sister. Moreover, the Parny family was involved in her baptism, her education, and her marriage in 1789.

Yet, despite Parny's story of ambivalent assimilation, in the very year of the publication of the *Chansons madécasses*, 1787, the poet wrote to his sister Javotte regarding an enslaved woman he owned called Auguste, asking for her to be sold.[16] We can set this against words Parny had written to his old friend Bertin in 1775: "Every day we trade a man for a horse: I find it impossible to get used to such a revolting and bizarre situation."[17] The cognitive dissonance, the compartmentalization, the sheer hypocrisy is astounding but surely not unusual for the era.

Despite his and his family's entrenchment in the slave economy on the Île Bourbon, Parny, like some slaveholding grandees in the America states such as Thomas Jefferson, maintained in his writings a theoretical Enlightenment opposition to the barbarity of the institution. If his grandfather had been a notorious hunter of escaped enslaved people, Parny himself expressed disgust at the practice. As he wrote to Bertin in 1775, "they go hunting for men as merrily as they would for blackbirds," adding that "a few make a successful escape from Île Bourbon back to Madagascar, but their countrymen massacred them, saying that they had come back from being among white people, and that they were too clever by half." Parny declares, in words that anticipate the opening cry of "Méfiez vous des blancs": "Unfortunate people! It's rather these very whites that you should be pushing from your peaceful shores."[18]

Parny could see the economic inefficiency of the system and also its moral bankruptcy, repeating the tale of a dying enslaved person who, coming to as he receives an involuntary baptism, declares that he doesn't want another life as even there he might perhaps still be enslaved by the person baptizing him. In his letters to Bertin, Parny refused the convenient fiction that enslaved men and women were not human beings, but his attitude was contradictory. He remained embedded in a social system founded on slavery.[19]

⊢

The *Chansons madécasses* can be seen as Parny's imaginative reaction to this moral morass, an attempt to engage with what he saw as both the humanity and the otherness of the enslaved people working as house servants, Malagasy by origin, among whom he lived, such as the nurse who brought him up or the women with whom he had intimate relations. Intriguingly, the voices he ventriloquizes in the *Chansons* are not those of Malagasy enslaved people on the Île Bourbon but free, fiercely resistant Malagasy on the as yet uncolonized island of Madagascar.

The *Chansons madécasses* are prose poems, poetic in nature but not written in verse. As perhaps the first prose poems in French, they were to have great literary influence on a long and distinguished tradition, and they made their mark on a whole generation of nineteenth-century poets, most notably Charles Baudelaire and Alexander Pushkin. Published in 1787 in France, they were printed with a frontispiece that fictitiously claimed they had been published on the Île Bourbon itself. The poems are presented as being translations of Malagasy originals, but it is clear that they were written by Parny himself. They have been shown nevertheless to be full of linguistic markers of documented accuracy, for example, in the use of names. Parny would have picked up some Malagasy as a child, and he retained a lifelong interest in this fascinating Austronesian language. The indigenous words for the power of the sun, *Zanhar*, and for a bad spirit, *ny angatra*, for example, are reflected in the deities Parny invokes in one of the songs not set by Ravel: "Zanahang and Niang." The name of the woman in Ravel's first, erotically charged song—the beautiful Nahandove for whom the speaker is waiting, with whom he makes love, and for whom on her departure he languishes—is derived from the indigenous word *nahandova*, "he who will inherit." Echoes of the rich tradition of Malagasy oral storytelling interact with European traditions. Parny's *Chansons madécasses* also included depictions of identifiable local social practices.

But in terms of external documentary evidence, the most

striking example is to be found in that second song set by
Ravel (actually song 5 of Parny's set) "Méfiez vous des blancs."
Here is the first part of the poem, in English:

> Beware of the white people, inhabitants of the shore.
>
> In the time of our fathers some white people descended
> on this island.
> They said to them: here's some land, let your women
> cultivate it.
> Be just, be good, and become our friends.
>
> The white people promised, and all the while they were
> making fortifications.
> A menacing fort was raised up.
> Thunder was encased in brass mouths.
> Their priests wanted to give us a God we didn't know.
> At last they spoke of obedience and slavery.
> Rather death.
>
> The carnage was long and terrible, but despite the
> lightning that they vomited and which wiped out
> whole armies, they were all exterminated.

This account clearly reflects French attempts at colonization
in the mid-seventeenth century—the efforts to deal with the
indigenous Malagasy, the erection of Fort Dauphin, the violence inflicted on the Malagasy, and the promulgation of the
Christian religion. The poem celebrates a French defeat.

When governor Étienne de Flacourt prepared to leave Fort
Dauphin in the 1650s (some twenty years before the final evac-
uation of the French settlement), he left behind a monument

recording his ignominious stay on the island. Repurposing a piece of marble left by earlier Portuguese settlers, he had inscribed on it three fleur-de-lis, as a symbol of the French monarchy, and this warning in Latin:

ADVENA

MONITA NOSTRA

TIBI TUIS VITAE

TUAE PROFUTURA

CAVE AB INCOLIS. VALE

Stranger, take heed of my warnings,
It will be profitable to you.
Beware of the inhabitants.
Farewell.[20]

In a powerful exercise of Enlightenment irony and a sure sign that, as well as knowing Madagascar's language and customs he knew the history of its relationship to French power, Parny inverted Flacourt's parting admonition. Beware of the inhabitants became beware of the white people. Distilling oral history picked up from nurses and lovers, Enlightenment opposition to the colonial project, and a working knowledge of Flacourt's vast book, the *Histoire de la Grande Isle Madagascar*, Parny created a unique protest against the aggressive designs of European settlers on the island of Madagascar. The final part of the poem makes it clear that Parny was not just writing history in condemnation of the seventeenth-century expedition under Flacourt but also contemporary commentary: we do well to remember that "Méfiez vous des blancs" was published just a year or less after the fatal shooting of the Baron Benyowski finally put an end to his crackpot, harebrained schemes for conquering Madagascar. This is clear from the following lines:

> We've seen new tyrants, stronger and more numerous,
> plant their flag on the shore.

> The sky fought for us, it made rains fall on them, storms
> and poisoned winds. They are no longer and we live
> free.

Parny's ventriloquism, and his adoption of an indigenous point of view, were by no means unprecedented among French writers of the eighteenth century. The abbé de Raynal's *Histoire des deux Indes* was first published in 1770, revised and expanded for a 1780 edition, and appeared in no less than forty-eight editions up to Raynal's death in 1796. The great Diderot collaborated with him on the book and contributed passages full of what the historian Jean-Michel Racault has called "the sanguinary lyricism of redeemed betrayal."[21] What makes Parny's work, and "Méfiez vous des blancs" in particular, so special, is his deep engagement with Malagasy culture and a fierce rhetorical stance that might almost seem to be fed by the guilt that must have afflicted Parny as slaveholder and colonialist. On one level, Parny's language seems to preempt that of the political philosopher and activist Frantz Fanon, born on Martinique, who spoke out against French colonial rule in Algeria in the 1960s. Here is Fanon at his most powerful:

> Their first encounter was marked by violence and their existence together—that is to say the exploitation of the native by the settler—was carried on by dint of a great array of bayonets and cannon. . . . In Indo-China, in Mada-

gascar or in the colonies the native has always known that he need expect nothing from the other side.... For the native life can only spring up out of the rotting corpse of the settler.... Illuminated by violence, the consciousness of the people rebels against any pacification.[22]

But, beneath the superficial similarities between Fanon's discursive practice and that of Parny, we need to locate Parny within his own historical moment in order to recognize both his precocious power and his lurking intellectual discomfort.

‒

If Parny's *Chansons madécasses* in general are based on the poet's intimate yet compromised interactions with the island and its people, its fifth song is grounded in identifiable historical events and recent attempts at conquest.

After Parny's day, Madagascar remained resistant to European settlement for another century, in many ways an icon of anticolonial resistance, in a world that was increasingly being divided up between the European powers. Informal colonial ventures were morphing into the formal colonial system negotiated at the Congress of Berlin, which was completed by the so-called scramble for Africa, into which Madagascar was anomalously drawn.

In the second and third decades of the nineteenth century, the highland kingdom of Imerina, a relatively weak force on the island, which had been hitherto challenged by more powerful coastal communities, came to dominate most of the island of Madagascar under the rule of Radama the Great. Radama was recognized as king of Madagascar by the British, but this recognition initiated a paradoxical process in which the unification of Madagascar under indigenous rule and efforts to create a nation-state on the European model were crucial in creating the conditions for a violent end to the long-term Malagasy resistance to European encroachment. Seesawing under succeeding monarchs between commercial entanglement with the European powers and an attempt to hold them and their Christianizing mission at bay, the Kingdom of Madagascar was drawn into the Anglo-French division of the colonial spoils. The Lambert charter, secretly concluded in 1855, gave the French exclusive rights to exploit land, natural resources, and projects, and it was as a result of attempts to revoke it that France eventually claimed Madagascar as a protectorate and, ultimately, in 1896 and with British acquiescence, as a colony.[23] Two wars were followed by a campaign of brutal pacification launched by General Joseph Gallieni. Leading Malagasy officials were shot by firing squad after show trials, and the queen of Madagascar, Ranavalona III, was sent into Algerian exile, dying in 1917. Madagascar was henceforth to be part of "la plus grande France."[24]

⊢

On May 24, 1925, some eight years after the death of the last queen of Madagascar, at a soiree to which the elite of the French musical establishment had been invited, a French mezzo-soprano named Jane Bathori stood up and, to the dissonant, brittle accompaniment of a pianist, a cellist, and a flute player, shrieked, twice, the mysterious exclamation "Aoua," before launching into Evariste Parny's words, in the fiercest of sung accents, "Méfiez-vous des blancs, habitans du rivage."[25]

That first performance of Ravel's song was part of an evening of chamber music commissioned by the American pianist and distinguished patron Elizabeth Sprague Coolidge. Coolidge commissioned a host of extraordinary pieces from the greatest composers—Britten, Copland, Prokofiev, Schoenberg, Stravinsky, Webern, Bartok, Respighi—but on that spring evening at the grand Majestic Hotel, it was Ravel's single sliver of a song that made the greatest impact. Of three *Chansons madécasses* that he had promised Coolidge earlier in the year, Ravel had only finished this one. It was a provocative promissory note for the entire cycle that would make its somewhat delayed debut the following year in Rome. "Aoua," as I'll call the song—an exclamation added to Parny's poem by Ravel—was the occasion for disturbance, if not quite on the level of the legendary Parisian riot that had attended the premiere of Stravinsky's *Rite of Spring* more than a decade earlier.

As the song ended, the Breton composer Léon Moreau got up and declared "M. Léon Moreau is leaving. He does not wish to listen again to such words while our country is fighting in Morocco." France was indeed pursuing a colonial war in North Africa at the time. Voices arose agreeing with Moreau's political objections, while others were quick to deplore the lack of politesse at this select event filled with distinguished invitees. Moreau and his supporters withdrew, and the song was repeated and enthusiastically received. The nascent public relations industry could not have conceived of an event more likely to whet the appetite for the *Chansons madécasses*, or to confirm Maurice Ravel's profile as a singularly radical force in French music.

The critic Arthur Hoerée reviewed Ravel's song in the October edition of the *Revue musicale*, and again in 1938 in a longer account of Ravel's lyrical output. He was intent on the severity of the work as opposed to the exoticism of earlier compositions by Ravel such as the song cycle *Shéhérazade*. Here was a clean and direct violence of expression that went hand in hand with an intense and shocking engagement with the bloody reality of the confrontation between the European and the Malagasy in a failed attempt at colonization. "He recounts to us the struggles of indigenous peoples against the white to win their freedom," Hoerée wrote in 1926. In 1938 he recalled this single song as "a hymn to liberty, against slavery [and] colonisation."[26]

Ravel had received the commission at his house in Montfort outside Paris, a house replete with the dandyish and ironically exoticizing elements that had up until then informed much of his music as well as his personal style. As one visitor put it, "We feel as if we are in a Chinese curio shop, in which a century of playful exoticism has been exposed."[27] Ravel's close friend Roland-Manuel described the arrival of the commission:

Being a confirmed admirer of bibelots dating back to the Revolution, Directoire, Empire and Restoration, Ravel bought, between an 1820 Gothic clock and an Etruscan teapot, a first edition of Evariste Parny. As he was looking through the poem Fleurs ... he had a cablegram from America from the 'cellist Kindler asking him to compose a song-cycle for Mrs Elisabeth [sic] S. Coolidge, with accompaniment "if possible" for flute, 'cello and piano. Always happy, in true Mozartian fashion, to adjust himself to another's will, the composer tenaciously went on reading Parny.... [He was] delighted by a peculiar, exotic quality which entirely suited his tastes, as local colour was virtually excluded.[28]

The image of Ravel projected through the account of his friend is that of the Baudelairean flaneur, the ironist, detached, amused: the Ravel we see in the dandyish man of the photographs of the 1920s. He sits in his charming salon reading the poems of Evariste Parny, but the poem he chooses to single out, the one he was reading just as the crucial telegram arrived, was not one he set and was a million miles from the aggressive protest of "Aoua." It was the ultra-aesthetic, quasi-erotic poem, "Les fleurs":

> The bulb prefers a thick luxurious soil.
> A light soil is sufficient for the seed,
> Entrust to it your tender hopes
> And of your flowers the delicate buds.[29]

Ravel was laconic about his own music, and the *Chansons madécasses* are no exception. He said not much more than this about them: "I think that the three Chansons Madécasses bring into being a new, dramatic, almost erotic element, resulting from the subject matter of Parny's poems."[30] This is teasing. The closest that Ravel comes to acknowledging the singular violence of "Aoua" is that word *dramatic*. He prefers, instead, to dwell on the atmosphere of the first and third poems of the set, which are surely not "almost" erotic but deeply charged with a heady eroticism. The first is nothing less than an evocation of anticipation, sexual fulfillment, and post-coital rest. In fact eroticism is not absent from Ravel's earlier works, like the song cycle *Shéhérazade*, with the orgasmic musical climax and postcoital nicotine haze of its first, ironically exotic song, "Asie," and the barely closeted homoerotic tension of the third, "L'indifférent." It was the political violence of "Aoua" that was shockingly new.

⊢

So, under this mask of quasi detachment, what were Ravel's politics? There's nothing systematic to go on; but what can be reconstructed from comments, allegiances, and occasional provocative acts?

In his friend Manuel Rosenthal's formulation, "Ravel never offered the slightest commentary on politics, none at all. He was what today would be called un homme de gauche, a man of the left, but he never expressed his opinions."[31]

At the outset of war in August 1914, Ravel wrote a letter to Cipa Godebski proclaiming "long life to the Internationale and Peace."[32] He went on to serve as a driver on the front, but in 1916 he aligned himself with those who saw the French nation and French culture as guarantors of universal values, refusing to join the nationalist Ligue pour la défense de la musique française.

Ravel subscribed to only one newspaper, a left-wing one, *Le populaire de Paris*, reading it attentively every day. In July 1925 André Gide set off to travel in the Congo, and it was in the *Populaire* that Leon Blum—a friend of Ravel's and socialist prime minister in 1936—flagged Gide's denunciations of the Congo concessionary companies and their human rights abuses in 1927, denunciations that were first published in the *Nouvelle revue française* in 1926 and that ultimately formed part of Gide's journal, *Voyage au Congo*, published in 1927.

Ravel would have met Gide at the salons of his close friends the Godebski family. He also attended the progressive Clemenceau salon, as did Albert Einstein and Stefan Zweig. In a period notorious for its intense antisemitism on the French right and in which the allegiances of the Dreyfus affair were persistent, Ravel had many Jewish friends, and he composed his *Mélodies hébraïques* in 1914, orchestrating them in 1920, the model of a cultural/political statement in oblique musical form—"political gestures through style," as the historian Jane Fulcher calls them.[33]

Ravel stood clearly apart from authority and the establishment; his dandyism was a declaration of intellectual independence, at one with a refusal, common in the period after the propaganda excesses of the war, to resort to using art as an overt form of political engagement. Hence he refused the Legion d'honneur in 1920. Was he somewhat embarrassed to be co-opted into a state apparatus of which he disapproved, or was he simply asserting his autonomy as an artist? The one does not, surely, exclude the other.

—

What was the political and cultural climate in the Paris that saw and heard that first shocking performance of the second of Ravel's *Chansons madécasses*? Léon Moreau's reference to the Moroccan war deserves attention. Morocco, under Sultan Yusef, had become a French protectorate in 1912, while a treaty signed in Madrid later the same year divided the country into four: a French administrative zone encompassing 90 percent of the country with its capital at Rabat; a small Spanish protectorate centered on Tetouan; a southern Saharan protectorate administered by the Spanish; and an international zone around Tangier. In June 1921 a rebellion in the Rif region in the mountainous northeast defeated a Spanish army of twenty-four thousand and proclaimed an independent state. French forces moved forward to defend their interests, and in April 1925 the Rif forces mounted an offensive against them. By July the newly appointed Marshal Pétain (victor of Verdun and later notorious figurehead of the collaborationist Vichy regime in the 1940s) made an agreement with the Spanish to pursue a unified strategy. This final stage of the Rif war lasted from autumn 1925 until spring 1926 and ended with the deportation of the Rif leader, Abd el-Krim, to the island of Réunion, where, of course, Parny had been born some two centuries earlier.

The Rif war was *the* political cause célèbre of 1925 in Paris, taken up by the surrealists as a renewing focus for political action and a way of discarding the Dadaist tendencies of the past, and by the newly formed French Communist Party as a way of distinguishing themselves from the anti-Bolshevik Section française de l'Internationale ouvrière (SFIO), led by Leon Blum, which had joined the government and remained committed to the notion of France's civilizing mission as a colonial power.[34] As Blum himself put it in July 1925,

> We acknowledge the right and even the duty of superior races to attract those who have not arrived at the same degree of culture and to call them to the progress realised thanks to the efforts of sciences and industry.... We have too much love for our country to disavow the expansion of its thought, of the French civilisation.[35]

Ministers of the SFIO were convinced that France had a duty to remain in Morocco, to protect its inhabitants, and to prevent what they characterized as an ominous descent into barbarism and Islamic fanaticism. Despite Blum's support for Gide's assault on the excesses of the colonial concessions in the Congo, the position of both men was that these were indeed excesses and that a distinction had to be maintained between criticizing colonial abuse and criticizing what they saw as the noble mission of colonialism (and the postwar mandate system) itself.

Ironically enough, it was Ravel's friend, Prime Minister Paul Painlevé, who escalated the war in Morocco in April 1925. In May the first of hundreds of antiwar demonstrations organized by the French Communist Party drew fifteen thousand protestors to the Parisian streets. It is not difficult to see why Ravel's four-minute-long song, with Parny's extraordinary anticolonial

message and a musical language of supremely laconic dissonant violence, was an agitprop bomb dropped into that fever-
ish May atmosphere. Ravel cannot have been unaware of the effect his song would have, but his subsequent comments about
the cycle, and the ultimate sandwiching of the violence of the
second song between two songs that depicted the more traditionally exoticist "attitudes de Plaisir et . . . abandon de la vo-
lupté,"[36] suggest a retreat back into his aestheticizing shell. The
Chansons madécasses were certainly a new venture for Ravel
aesthetically, and the violence of the second song is a brilliant
musical foil for the languor of the first and third. But the shocking political context should not be allowed simply to evapo-
rate.

According to the historian Jane Fulcher, Ravel's ideological
practice was a matter of "subversion [that] was always subtle,
taking place on the level of symbols and gestures which, as he
well knew, could be even more powerful than conventional
discursive confrontation."[37] If the second song of the *Chansons madécasses* is not a political manifesto, and is layered
with as many ideological complexities as Parny's poems, its
"subversion" is surely more than "subtle," being rather an exercise in imaginative identification with the "other" that prob-
lematizes or questions—as art surely can and should—the
orthodoxies of the political and social order. Nevertheless, as
a work of ventriloquism, like Parny's poems, it remains prob-
lematic.[38] Who should speak for the oppressed, then and now,
for those who have been silenced? And to what extent was
Ravel's song an expression of radical chic?

▬

As part of French culture's engagement with the colonial
"other," Parny and Ravel's vision of Madagascar and acts of
ventriloquism may be troubling, but it's undeniable that

"Méfiez vous des blancs," as song or prose poem, was a radical anticolonial intervention and was received as such by some audience members at its premiere.

Poulenc's *Rapsodie nègre* shows us how very different a twentieth-century French composer's engagement with the idea of Madagascar could be. During the war, in 1917, Ravel was present at the première. The piece was, Poulenc later disingenuously wrote, "a reflection of the taste for African art that has flourished since 1912 under the impetus of Apollinaire." The baritone scheduled to sing at the first performance withdrew at the last moment, Poulenc explained, "saying it was all too stupid . . . [so] I had to sing this interlude myself, partially obscured by a huge music stand. As I had already been mobilised one can imagine the unexpected effect of this soldier bawling in pseudo-Malagasy."[39]

This poem was, in fact, part of an offensive racist imposture, *Les poésies de Makoko Kangourou*. This collection of poems by a (fictitious) Liberian author had been published in 1910. Most were written in ungrammatical and syntactically challenged French, but a nonsense poem, "Honoloulou," supposedly in the poet's own language, was included, and this is what Poulenc set as the third movement of the *Rapsodie*. The poems were ostensibly edited, with a spurious apparatus of footnotes, by Marcel Prouille and Charles Moulié (pseudonyms of Marcel Ormoy and Thierry Sandre). The fictitious Kangourou is supposedly feted in his own country, and the book is tricked out with a nasty frontispiece showing the poet as a stereotypical African savage comically adorned with a laurel wreath and wearing a toga. Ravel's typically laconic yet possibly sarcastic comment on *Rapsodie nègre* was that Poulenc had "created his own folklore."

⊢

Poulenc's work shows the most offensive side of what at the time in Paris was known as *négrophilie* or "negrophilia." As Petrine Archer-Straw, the historian and author of a pioneering study of the phenomenon, puts it, "Not black culture in and for itself, but black culture as an interlude to modernity." At its most egregious, "blacks were packaged exotically for the market-place at the same time that race theories defend them as lesser beings."[40] Josephine Baker, star of the Revue nègre and later an American civil rights activist, deftly encapsulated the problem: "The white imagination sure is something when it comes to blacks."[41] Mid-1920s Parisian culture at one and the same patronized and celebrated black artists: the crucial contradiction lay in an attitude that, in continuity with the prewar avant-garde, questioned the self-satisfied conviction of white Europe's material and moral progress but did so by asserting the alternative value system of a so-called primitive or uncivilized blackness of the imagination.[42]

It is important to recognize that this is the cultural moment from which Ravel's song emerged. Ravel was undoubtedly participating in the vogue that was "negrophilia" while at the same time issuing a powerful and unmistakable cry against the horrors of colonialism. Layer on layer of progressive intentions, bad faith, and inconvenient not to say corrupting material and political entanglements underlie Parny's original prose poems. The context of Ravel's masterpiece is just as complex.

▬

I first heard the *Chansons madécasses* in a powerful and singularly beautiful performance by the British born Afro-Caribbean mezzo-soprano Ruby Philogene at the Wigmore Hall on July 11, 1995. It has haunted my memory ever since.

I talked to Philogene about the piece, and her relationship to it, more than a quarter of a century later. She spoke of feeling a particular connection to it, and especially to the second song, and of sensing the presence of her enslaved forebears on the Caribbean island of Dominica, of their experiences of oppression, with echoes of their linguistic heritage—French remained current in Dominica long after its cession to the British by the French in 1763. Both sides of Philogene's family are from Dominica; one ancestor on her father's side was a white French plantation owner (Philogène is a French name). Philogene can "feel my ancestors sounding through me in my interpretation: their cry of oppression, their cry of injustice for liberty." She delivered the second song as what she spoke of as a "wake-up call": "don't sleepwalk through this" was how she put it to me, as if the song had the power to connect a contemporary audience with the history of resistance to enslavement and its continuing implications in the present. Incidentally and intriguingly, Philogene told me that that opening cry of "Aoua," which Ravel added to Parny's prose poem, sounds like a local Caribbean expression, meaning something like "don't stand a chance" or "not a hope." This adds another ambiguous performative layer, another possibility for the mysterious opening of Ravel's setting of Parny's fifth chanson.[43]

Authenticity is the holy grail of sung performance, but it can mean many things. The authenticity of Philogene's performance in 1995—the authenticity she describes feeling in performing that second song and that I sensed as a member of the audience—came from a deep and very personal sense of identification with its story of oppression and with its cry for liberation. It was a performance in which she made the song her own, at one and the same time embodying and

transcending the historical experiences so ambiguously encoded in Parny's poem and Ravel's music.

I've performed the cycle only once, in Italy in 2018. It was
a fascinating experience, with an international group of musicians of great capacity and imagination—Emmanuel Pahud
(flute), Christian Poltéra (cello) and Lucille Chung (piano).
The abstract appeal of the music was gripping and energizing;
yet at the same time, I've learned these extraordinary songs
cannot really be experienced, by performers or audience, in
the abstract. The drama of the second song is compelling, but
to have a white European sing it and embody the political history of which it speaks seems oddly of a piece with the awk-
wardnesses and compromised progressiveness of the poet
Parny and the composer Ravel themselves. Layers on layers.

"The tradition of all the dead generations," Marx wrote
in his *18th Brumaire of Louis Bonaparte* (1852), "weighs like
a nightmare on the brain of the living."[44] The play of identity in which all singers engage is enabled and constrained
by the accumulated strata of historical events and ideological constructions and by the circumstances of our own lives.
Should I be performing these songs? Do I have the right to do
so? How does my identity relate to the many selves on offer
in the words and the music? Or to the identity of composer
or poet? Or to the Malagasy people of the eighteenth century,
so powerfully yet problematically ventriloquized by Parny.
I don't know. What I do know is that addressing the hidden
history of this piece intensifies and complicates our response
to it, as performers and as audience.

3

"These Fragments Have I Shored against My Ruins"

Meditations on Death

eath is not only the ultimate dissolution of identity, as all the physical, psychological, and social ligatures that tether it in place are severed; it is also that in the face of which we make our identity. "These fragments have I shored against my ruins," as T. S. Eliot put it in *The Waste Land* (1922). Habits, interests, love, the hourly, the daily, and all the busi-ness of life. Above all, art.

It was the philosopher Bernard Williams who argued, in a famous essay on Janacek's opera *The Makropulos Case*—about a woman gifted, or rather cursed, with immortality—that life only makes sense in the face of its finitude. "We are lucky in having the chance to die," Williams concluded. This does not require that death itself be desirable: death can destroy meaning while at the same time the prospect of mortality creates the very meaning that death destroys. That, at least, is one reading of Williams's long and complex argument.

It is somehow appropriate that Williams's discussion centers on an opera. This is not just because Janacek's *Makropulos Case* is about the daughter of a court physician in the sixteenth century who, having taken an elixir of life, is now 342 years old and, consequently, "in a state of boredom, indifference and coldness."[1]

Music is expressive without being denotative. It is material and precise but at the same time metaphysically suggestive, the closest thing this side of revelation to a glimpse of the divine. It is in music that this paradox of Williams's can be contained and engaged with; that which creates meaning also destroys it. Music helps us to deal with death, with its inevitability, its incomprehensibility, its necessity. In certain pieces of music we face death within a world of sounds that is resolutely alive at the same time as it is transitory, fleeting, and always decaying. Music has, in Shakespeare's words, a dying fall.

Silence is the ultimate symbol of death in terms of sound, but "until we die," as John Cage, composer of the notoriously silent *4'33"* supposedly had it, "there will be sounds." Utter soundlessness, true silence, is not available to the living subject.

Gestures towards silence, however, are part of our cultural encounter, while we remain alive, with the nothingness of death — our own horror vacui, that sense of emptiness and loss that we feel in the face of the death of others, or the peace and calm that silence seems to offer.

This relative silence, this imagined silence, can be an evocation of things that are inexpressible. There is that organized and audible silence with which many societies mourn their dead: the silence at a funeral, the two-minute silence observed in memory of the war dead since the end of the First World War. These silences encourage us to think of the departed, to memorialize them, but they also necessarily and inevitably involve thinking about our own mortality. They bind together the living and the dead in a contemplation of a common end.

Silence is essential to music, the rests as important as the notes. But beyond that, in classical music's engagement with finality, with death, there are especially significant silences that gesture towards nothingness. I think especially of a song in Schubert's great cycle for voice and piano *Winterreise*, twenty-four songs, written in 1827/1828. This work was composed in the face of impending death. Schubert had contracted syphilis in 1823, and although his death, in 1828, came early and unexpectedly, possibly from typhus, he spent the last five years of his life under the shadow of an early demise, producing works in his last eighteen months that seem to speak to a sense of mortality. *Winterreise* is a journey into the snow, white blankness, a journey away from a failed love affair in which the journeyer looks deeply into himself and, plumbing the depths of loneliness and isolation, metaphysical despair. He learns a lesson that Samuel Beckett (who loved the cycle) took up in the twentieth century: "You must go on. I can't go on. I'll go on" is how his novel *The Unnamable* ends.

In the fourteenth song in *Winterreise*, "Der greise Kopf" (The old man's head), the wanderer discovers that the frost has turned his hair white. The music in the piano expresses a sort of horror at this transformation, with a leap of an augmented fourth, that unholy interval that late medieval musicians christened the *diabolus in musica*. The wanderer reacts with an expression of grim satisfaction: one step closer to the end of his journey, the journey we all take towards death. Then the frost melts, and our hero is a young man again—

"How far it is still to the grave!" (Wie weit noch bis zur Bahre!). Schubert's repetition of this statement at a lower pitch, barely harmonized, is followed by a pause that, when I perform the cycle, always seems to demand a longer than usual duration, an extended, unnatural, almost unmusical silence in which Schubert, the musicians, and the audience look into the abyss. And if we want to understand this biographically—which is to say, to understand it as the expression of a suffering human being, Franz Schubert, rather than a creator genius—it is as if Schubert is repeating the phrase not to underline our distance from dissolution but to grasp its inevitability and to contemplate our own mortality. Silence points deathward here.

Schubert had a particular gift for what we might call deathly music even before his illness. One of his earliest songs, never completed, is called "Leichenfantasie," corpse fantasy; another song, a miraculous setting of a poem by Goethe, "Wandrers Nachtlied," is a paradoxical evocation of stillness through a particular sort of quiet music:

Über allen Gipfeln ist Ruh,
In allen Wipfeln spürest du
Kaum einen Hauch.
Die Vöglein schweigen im Walde.
Balde ruhest du auch.

Over every mountain top is quiet,
In each and every treetop you can
hardly feel a breath.
The birds are silent in the woods.
Soon you too will be quiet. (Translation mine)

The instrumental music that Schubert wrote in the last years of his life is not all drenched in contemplation of mortality—

there's a lot of dance music for piano, for example, an excellent distraction, surely, from morbid thoughts. But many of the late works, while anything but morbid, seem to speak to the listener as intimations and explorations of the evanescence of human life and the ever present defining limit that is death. Here is the critic and philosopher George Steiner in his book *Real Presences* struggling to express these ideas, which are so hard to get a handle on:

> What we can say, a saying both exceeding and falling short of responsible knowledge, is that there is music which conveys both the grave constancy, the finality of death and a certain refusal of that very finality. This dual motion, instinctual to humanity but scandalous to reason, is evident, it is made transparent to spiritual, intellectual and physical notice, in Schubert's C-major Quintet. Listen to the slow movement.[2]

—

Benjamin Britten is a composer who grappled, throughout his career, with the horror and inevitability of death in music of transcendent power. His meditations on death are some of the most profound that we have, at the same time troubling and consoling. Starting with his first symphony, titled *Sinfonia da Requiem*, he put death very publicly at the center of his output from early on in his career as a composer.

In 1939, a few weeks after the outbreak of the Second World War, he had received an unusual commission from the Japanese government: he was asked to compose a symphony to celebrate the 2,600th anniversary of the founding of the Mikado dynasty. Britten, a known pacifist, was an odd choice for the militaristic Japanese regime, but Britten undiplomatically doubled down: "I'm making it as anti-war as possible," he told a New York newspaper in April 1940. His friend the composer Lennox Berkeley found the choice of Britten for a commission from a nation that was currently executing a vicious war in China "a piece of disconcerting irony." The piece that resulted was the *Sinfonia da Requiem*. Not only was it publicly trailed as an antiwar piece, it was also structured in three parts, each given the title from the Roman Catholic mass for the dead. In the end, perhaps inevitably, the Japanese government withdrew the commission: "Mr Benjamin Britten's composition is so very different from the anticipation of the committee."

What did Britten intend in the first place? Could the *Sinfonia* have been, as Britten's latest biographer Paul Kildea suggests, a sort of "Trojan horse," an antiwar piece smuggled into the Japanese celebrations? This seems unlikely, given Britten's recklessly unguarded public remarks about the piece. He was certainly annoyed to have had the commission withdrawn, and it seems, therefore, that it was an unexpected outcome. His political bravado was something he expected, perhaps foolishly, to get away with. He could have presented the piece to the Japanese without controversial public comment; but, ultimately, a piece structured as a *Requiem* offered to celebrate the immortality of a divine and ancient dynasty was a more than disconcerting choice.

Dedicated to his deceased parents, the *Sinfonia da Requiem* consists of three movements, each imagined as a section from the ancient requiem mass for the dead: a Lacrimosa, lamenting; a Dies irae, fearful, nervous; a Requiem aeternam, pleading for eternal rest. As a piece of abstract music, often Mahlerian in quality, it escapes from Britten's political agenda and retains the metaphorical freedom that allows it to be at one and the same time a protest at the slaughter of war, a musical manifesto for peace, and a personal reckoning with mortality in the tradition of the great requiems of the past—those of Mozart, Verdi, Fauré. The dedication to his late parents is a measure of the work's intensely personal core.³

—

Britten spent the early years of the war in the United States, where he wrote the *Sinfonia da Requiem*, but he returned to England in 1942, undertaking the dangerous wartime Atlantic crossing. He flung himself into writing some of his greatest pieces, including his opera *Peter Grimes*, and giving concerts as part of his war work as a registered conscientious objector. He was working now almost exclusively with words. There was *Grimes*; his song cycle in Italian, the *Seven Sonnets of Michelangelo*; his anthology of English verse, the *Serenade for Tenor, Horn and Strings*, which in its keening and creepy fourth song, the "Lyke Wake Dirge," confronts death head on. Britten developed a new and muscular approach to the setting of English poetry, earnest for intelligibility but also unafraid of melisma, returning to the inspiration of England's greatest composer of the seventeenth century, Henry Purcell.

In July 1945, the war in Europe recently over, Britten was invited to a party hosted by his English publishers, Boosey and Hawkes. There he met that most celebrated of violinists, Yehudi Menuhin. Menuhin had offered his services to a Jewish group that was working together with the United Nations and planning to travel to war-ravaged Germany with the pianist Gerald Moore to play together for survivors of the Bergen-Belsen camp in Lower Saxony and for German civilians in the surrounding area, "the saddest ruins of the Third Reich" as Menuhin put it later. As Menuhin remembered, "[It was just a week] before I was going to go to Germany to play for the displaced persons at the camps. Ben desperately wanted to go at all costs. . . . and indeed Ben came with us."

Britten replaced Gerald Moore as Menuhin's accompanist.

This was to be Britten's last job as a conscientious objector, affiliated to what was known as ENSA, the Entertainments National Service Association. The interaction between this trip and his conscience can only have been a complex one, since he had refused to fight. "Two, & sometimes three concerts a day" were presented, Britten wrote, to listeners "in, some of them, appalling states, who could scarcely sit still & listen, and yet were thrilled to be played for." "Men and women alike, our audience was dressed in army blankets fashioned by clever tailors among them into skirts and suits. No doubt a few weeks since their rescue they had put a little flesh on their bones, but to our unaccustomed eyes they seemed desperately haggard, and many were still in hospital."

The cellist Anita Lasker-Wallfisch, a Holocaust survivor, was present at these concerts and wrote about them much later:

Concerning the accompanist, I can only say that I just can not imagine anything more beautiful [or] wonderful. Somehow one never noticed that there was any accompanying going on at all, and yet I had to stare at this man like one transfixed as he sat seemingly suspended between chair and keyboard, playing so beautifully.

Pressed in the 1960s to describe how this experience in Germany in 1945 had been, Britten could only say "we gave two or three short recitals a day—they couldn't take more. It was in many ways a terrifying experience." After Britten's death, his partner, the tenor Peter Pears, said "that the experience had coloured everything he had written subsequently."

On his return to London, Britten plunged headlong and feverishly (quite literally, as he was suffering from the after-effects of a typhoid inoculation) into the composition of one of his greatest song cycles, *The Holy Sonnets of John Donne*, in which death is at the forefront. His previous cycle for voice and piano, the *Seven Sonnets of Michelangelo*, had been an extraordinarily brave and explicit declaration of love for his partner, and the first singer of the cycle, Peter Pears, even if it had been a declaration of his sexuality concealed behind the Renaissance complexities of Michelangelo's poetic language. In choosing to set the poetry of Donne, Britten was turning from the sixteenth to the seventeenth century, from mannered Italian to metaphysical English, from love to a confrontation with death and sin. The cycle was completed on August 19, 1945, ten days after the second atomic bomb was dropped on the Japanese city of Nagasaki, bringing the war in the Pacific to an end. The cycle was written in the shadow of horror. It was performed by Britten and Pears at the Wigmore Hall on November 22.[4]

⊢

The poet and divine John Donne's relationship with death was complex, anxious, and obsessive, full of contradiction, tainted by heterodoxy. In 1608 he wrote the first treatise justifying suicide in English, *Biathanatos*. A shocking work for its time and not published until after his death, it even implied that Jesus Christ himself committed suicide. Yet by 1615 Donne had embarked on a stellar career as a minister in the Church of England, committed to orthodoxy, rising to become Dean of St. Paul's Cathedral in 1621. His confrontations with the inevitability of extinction are startlingly intense in character. A few weeks before his death, a portrait was made of him clothed in his own shroud. And he was famous for having delivered his own funeral sermon not long before his death, poised as he

FIGURE 5. Martin Droeshout, *John Donne*, 1633. Line engraving. © National Portrait Gallery, London.

was on "the lips of that whirlpool, the grave," in Lent 1630.[5] It was published not long after as "Death's Duell."

In the "Hymn to God the Father," a poem that Pears and Britten particularly loved,[6] Donne berates himself for his many sins, ending, crucially, with "a sinne of feare, that when I have spunne / My last thred, I shall perish on the shore":[7] a fear that death is indeed the end of everything and that the crossing over from earth to eternity is nothing but an illusion. This was for Donne an admission of sin, of an unorthodox questioning of the doctrine of the afterlife; but it also powerfully expressed his personal and visceral resistance to nothingness, to extinction, the sense that these could be worse even than the horrors of damnation.

The Holy Sonnets—both Donne's and Britten's—are anything but quiet and resigned. They are noisy, terrified, terrifying. As the critic John Carey has noted, "the prospect of annihilation . . . was highly antipathetic to Donne. His aim, when he writes about death, is to make it more active and positive than life, and so negate its deathliness."[8] But that underlying and basic fear of extinction is harnessed to the orthodox Protestant fear of eternal damnation as the wages of sin—the theme that runs through most of Donne's nineteen *Holy Sonnets*. And while a sort of panic-ridden energy courses through much of Donne's extraordinary and extravagant language, it is an energy contained within the form of the sonnet, hitherto used almost exclusively for the poetry of love.

Among the nine sonnets Britten chooses to set to music are some of Donne's most anguished poems. This, for example (Sonnet 1):

Thou hast made me, And shall thy worke decay?
Repaire me now, for now mine end doth haste,

I runne to death, and death meets me as fast,
And all my pleasures are like yesterday,
I dare not move my dimme eyes any way,
Despaire behind, and death before doth cast
Such terrour, and my feeble flesh doth waste
By sinne in it, which it t'wards hell doth weigh;
Onely thou art above, and when towards thee
By thy leave I can looke, I rise againe
But our old subtle foe so tempteth me,
That not one houre my selfe I can sustaine,
Thy Grace may wing me to prevent his art,
And thou like Adamant draw mine iron heart.[9]

The fear that Donne summons up here—"I runne to death, and death meets me as fast"—is brilliantly conveyed by Britten as the fingers of the pianist seem to chase each other across the keyboard in a moto perpetuo dance of death. The voice states its challenge to its maker—"Thou hast made me, And shall thy worke decay?"—and then participates in the scurrying terror that the piano has set up. As the poem briefly looks towards God, the voice and piano are suspended in an ethereal upper register, but the song ends with a coda in the piano of surpassing brutality, chords that seem to want to crush thought. There is something visceral about this song, the expression of a personal and overwhelming fear of death, regardless of the theological niceties of the poem itself, with its offer of redeeming grace.

The songs as a whole are a juxtaposition and alternation of intense keening, energy, violence, and fear. In the center, emotionally if not literally, is an oasis: the sonnet Donne wrote on the death of his wife in 1617, "Since she whom I loved," which Britten sets with an aching rhythm, two in the voice against three in the piano, difficult in practice to sustain at such a slow tempo and which seems to embody the yearning of loss. Private and public are continually interwoven in this cycle. Britten's feverishness in the summer of 1945, which seems to inform much of the character of the cycle, is announced at the outset, as the poet is "summoned by sicknesse, death's herald, and champion," and it returns with the "fantastique ague" of the fourth song, "O to vex me." On the public plane there is talk of tyrannies, dearth, prison, execution, war—words that would have had a particular resonance for an audience in 1945 and for a man, the composer, who had been witness to the consequences of the darkest horrors of the Nazi regime. There is a sustained interplay in the songs between notions of sin, repentance, grace, pardon, and forgiveness that straddle the realms of the personal and the societal in the wake of war and of extermination. It is difficult to hear the words of song five, "What if this present were the world's last night," without thinking of the horrific destructiveness of war and of the recent obliterations of Hiroshima and Nagasaki.

The last song of the *Holy Sonnets* is perhaps the most famous poem of the set—"Death be not proud." For the critic John Carey, "part of the strength of this poem [is] that its argument is so weak. Its ill assorted reasons tumble out in no recognizable order, reflecting inner disarray."[10] Donne's sonnet form tames this disorder, and while Britten's settings of Donne often disrupt or obscure the metrical design of the verse, the music he composes for this song, in a similar way to the sonnet form, holds the disarray at an emotional distance. Compared to the other songs of the cycle, this one pulsates with an ominous calmness. The music Britten composes for this song is a passacaglia with a five-bar ground bass: essentially variations over an ostinato pattern that creates a sense of timelessness. It is stately, assured, calm. Even the references to fate, chance, kings, desperate men, poison, "warre," and "sicknesse"—to all of which death is a slave—have a sort of detached grandeur. As so often in the song repertoire, formal analysis of the song tells us one thing, performance another, because the words and the music exist in tension with each other. Britten does not *set* the words to music but offers a commentary on them that in its detachment only intensifies the inadequacy of this catalog of challenges to death's dominion. When those famous final words ring out, sustained, in self-contradictory defiance—"Death thou shalt die"—they ring hollow.

Donne's *Holy Sonnets* are an expression of the paradoxes and tensions that are created in a mind psychologically and poetically alive to death: they are poems that are, as John Carey notes, the product of a powerful ego that cannot accept the inevitability of its own demise. Britten crafts from them something which certainly engages with that self-centered anxiety; but, intended to be performed in public, and to be performed by two men who were deep colleagues and devoted lovers, it already moves on a different plane, in several ways.

That central song, not arithmetically but emotionally—"Since she whom I loved"—the song on the death of Donne's wife, has words that tell, despite Donne's grief, of the poet's continued focus on the issue of his own redemption. "Why should I beg more love" from God, he writes, punning on his wife's surname (she was born Anne More); and her role in the sonnet is to lead him to God. Britten's music pushes it very much in another direction, filling it with a tremendous warmth of generous love that reminds us of the equally still and rapturous third song of his Michelangelo sonnets, an unabashed love song.

More importantly, the cycle as a whole, drenched as it is

in sin and death, must surely have spoken to its audience in late autumn 1945 as a meditation on and a reckoning with the horrors of six years of total war. This is something Britten finds again and again in his music: an elision of the public and the private vision of death, a visceral grappling with its personal meaning but also with its public context. At the same time, what lies buried at the heart of Britten's cycle—to be experienced by any voice and piano duo who perform it and then transmitted to the audience—is a rare and frightening experience of guilt, the complex guilt Britten must have felt as a noncombatant after witnessing Bergen-Belsen postliberation, and of justified rage, as a pacifist, seeing evidence of the horrendous destructiveness of modern warfare in the area around it. This inevitable tension feeds the cycle. It makes it all the more striking that in the great public work he wrote to mourn and commemorate the Second World War, his *War Requiem* of 1962, neither Nazi extermination nor the war from the air are directly addressed.

Britten's *Holy Sonnets* have an epilogue, a complete draft in pencil setting a piece of prose by Donne, the seventeenth "Meditation" from the *Devotions upon Emergent Occasions*, with its supremely famous phrase (immortalized by Ernest Hemingway), "for whom the bell tolls."[11] It was struck out in Britten's manuscript and never published or, apparently, sung, until it was rediscovered after the composer's death. Here is the text Britten set:

PERCHANCE he for whom this bell tolls may be so ill, as that he knows not it tolls for him;

The bell doth toll for him that thinks it doth; and though it intermit again, yet from that minute that this occasion wrought upon him, he is united to God.

Who bends not his ear to any bell which upon any
occasion rings? but who can remove it from that bell
which is passing a piece of himself out of this world? No
man is an island, entire of itself; every man is a piece of
the continent, a part of the main.

If a clod be washed away by the sea, Europe is the less,
as well as if a promontory were, as well as if a manor
of thy friend's or of thine own were: any man's death
diminishes me, because I am involved in mankind, and
therefore never send to know for whom the bell tolls; it
tolls for thee.[12]

Britten's setting is particularly striking because, as a setting
for the voice, it is barely a setting at all. The piano starts the
piece with octave F♯'s, repeated three times, *sempre mezzo piano*. These repeated notes continue throughout the piece as
the voice enters on that same note, F♯, freely intoning, chant-
ing, speaking the text, quasi parlando, all on F♯, with the piano
adding a largely chordal accompaniment. The *mezzo piano*
F♯'s in the piano continue relentlessly throughout the piece.

This repeated motif is clearly the tolling bell of Donne's
"Meditation," insistent and admonitory. It encodes the social
and the personal, for while the "Meditation" is a reminder that
we are all connected, that we are all parts of each other, that
any death diminishes us, it also encapsulates the recognition
associated with any act of mourning another—a funeral, the
two minutes silence—that this is our common destination.
"Ask not for whom the bell tolls, it tolls for thee." The public
and the private intertwined, the social and the personal.

This epilogue is a brilliant structural/compositional ma-
neuver by Britten, because in the tolling bells of the epilogue,

the hammering, fierce octaves at the outset of the cycle—
the first sonnet, "O my blacke soule"—are retrospectively revealed to be bells, too, if singularly ferocious ones. These are
bells that in this opening sonnet are the summons of sickness,
"death's herald and champion." And in the "Meditation" with
which Britten originally made to close his cycle, Donne is confined to bed with a dangerous fever, and it is the noise of the
"passing bell" tolling to mark the dying of a neighbor that elic-
its his reflections. Like Donne, Britten, too, as we know, had
been confined to bed with a fever while writing.

And so this muted setting of the "Meditation" weaves together Britten's personal state and a public declaration of sol-
idarity with the suffering of liberated Europe. We can only
speculate as to why he excised it. It may be simply that the
epilogue is too explicit in its connection of the preceding
cycle with Britten's condition and the condition of Europe.
There's perhaps an awkwardness there, an embarrassment or
discomfort expressed in Britten's refusal to talk much about
what he had experienced in Germany in 1945. The terror and
compassion, the guilt and the fury of *The Holy Sonnets of John
Donne* in their final form stand alone, without explanation,
to circulate in the realm of the metaphorical—which doesn't
stop us speculating on their origins.

▬

Those passing bells that called to Donne on his sick bed return in Britten's greatest public work of mourning, his *War
Requiem*, composed for the reconsecration of the bombed
out Coventry Cathedral in 1962. Already before the commission, Britten had been talking about his plans for "a Mass . . .
a rather sad 20th century, European affair," so the call from
Coventry in October 1958 was perfectly timed. It was an idea

that came from within but that was ultimately crafted as a very prominent and public commission. He was writing the piece both for himself and for the world at large.

The whole piece embodies a dialogue between the private and the public, as it alternates between a large scale and musically allusive setting of the requiem mass for soprano soloist, double choir, and symphony orchestra (Requiem aeternam, Dies irae, Offertorium, Sanctus, Agnus dei, and Libera me), and settings of war poems by Wilfred Owen for baritone and tenor and chamber orchestra, written in Britten's most personal and hermetic style. The whole mass starts with tolling bells, F♯ (a subliminal echo of the Donne cycle?) and then C, a tritone, the notorious *diabolus in musica*, or "devil in music." Something is not quite right. The first of the Owen settings is his "Anthem for Doomed Youth"—"what *passing bells* for these who die as cattle" (my emphasis), passing bells that may remind us of that Donne "Meditation" that Britten had abortively set some twenty years earlier.

Britten's choice of the First World War poet Wilfred Owen was especially brilliant. Of all the war poets, it was Owen who was able to modulate the tropes and linguistic idiosyncrasies of the English religious tradition; this in turn allows his poetry to stand in ironic counterpoint to the text of the Latin requiem mass. Hence, those tolling bells opening the piece are matched by the passing bells of "Anthem for Doomed Youth"—which are no bells indeed but only "the monstrous anger of the guns" or the "rifles' rapid rattle." The "tuba mirum spargens sonum" (trumpet pouring forth its awful sound) of the Dies irae disperses into the "bugles . . . saddning the evening air" of Owen's unfinished poem, "But I was looking at the permanent stars." The grandeur—or is it bluster?—of "Rex tremendae majestatis" (King of fearful majesty) tumbles into the music hall knockabout of Britten's setting of "The Next War" ("Out there we've walked quite friendly up to death"), in which the two soldierly comrades, tenor and baritone, laugh at death, their "old chum." Mention of God's promise to Abraham and his seed, the promise of eternal life, in the Offertorium, is matched by Owen's refashioning of the Old Testament story of Abraham and Isaac. Britten had already set a medieval mystery play version of Abraham and Isaac in his Canticle 2 for tenor, alto, and piano. It is a familiar tale, if a perplexing one: God asks Abraham to offer his son Isaac as a sacrifice, but at the last minute, happy with Abraham's obedience, relents. Britten reuses some of the music from that piece in this setting, but in Owen's retelling, the punchline is a grim and devastatingly ironic one—the old man refuses to accept God's last minute offer of mercy and "slew his son, and half the seed of Europe one by one."

Britten's *War Requiem*, despite all those devastating ironies of juxtaposition, is not a simple act of antiestablishment pacifism. It is full of the paradoxes that all great works of art contain, and while Britten was insistent on its pacifist message, it cannot be reduced to a series of propagandistic commonplaces—war is bad, governments that fight wars are laced with hypocrisy. Doubtless true; but reducing the *Requiem* to such self-evident simple nostrums eviscerates its ambiguous power.

Here is a piece commissioned to commemorate the destruction of Coventry Cathedral during the Second World War that is grounded in the sounds and experiences of trench warfare in the First World War. Genocide and aerial bombardment are avoided—though Britten did, late in his life, write a devastating response to the war from the air, his setting of William Soutar's "The Children," from the cycle *Who Are These*

Children? (1969): "The blood of children stares from the broken stone."[13]

And, through all this, it has to be remembered that Owen himself was not a pacifist and fought on, to be killed just a week before the Armistice in November 1918. In his copy of Edmund Blunden's 1931 memoir of Owen, a preface to a collection of his poems, Britten highlighted this passage:

> Already I have comprehended a light which never will filter into the dogma of any national church: namely that one of Christ's essential commands was: Passivity at any price! Suffer dishonour and disgrace, but never resort to arms. Be bullied, be outraged, be killed; but do not kill. It may be chimerical and an ignominious principle, but there it is. It can only be ignored; and I think pulpit professionals are ignoring it very skilfully and successfully indeed. . . . And am I not myself a conscientious objector with a very seared conscience.[14]

That seems to be a most apt summary of the tension powering so much of Britten's work—"a conscientious objector with a very seared conscience"—Owen's conscience seared because he fought and killed, Britten's because he did not.

Britten's *War Requiem* is a piece with which I feel a very strong connection. I performed it first as part of an act of remembrance, in 1994, before I was even a professional singer—in Guildford, England, and Freiburg, Germany, to commemorate the fiftieth anniversary of the bombing of Freiburg in November of 1944. Since then I have performed it some eighty-four times—three times in 2002 with the Chicago Symphony under Mstislav Rostropovich, husband of Galina Vishnevskaya, for whom the soprano part was written. So, I have sat through the piece, in concert and rehearsal, many,

many times. It is difficult, of course, to sum up a reaction to such a piece in mere words, but my feeling each time—apart from the indestructible nature of the *Requiem*, its quality of sustained intensity and ability to move and engage performers and orchestra—is that this enormous and impressive structure, this very public piece, nevertheless nurses at its core the same personal and private preoccupations that animate a piece like the *Holy Sonnets*. The *War Requiem* is a commemorative piece, but its mourning for the lost dead is only amplified by the sadness and terror of the transience of human life and that guilt at our inevitable complicity in suffering, which it reiterates at each performance. The personal and the interpersonal relentlessly and expressively intertwined.

⊢

It goes without saying that all the music that Benjamin Britten wrote was meant for public performance, but it could be more or less public in feeling and aesthetic, more or less intimate in style or scoring, more or less encoded with private thoughts, fears, tensions, guilts, or embarrassments. The *War Requiem* is full of such secrets no doubt, more or less buried, but it was surely the most public piece Britten ever wrote. The nature of the commission, the degree of public scrutiny, the large sales of the LP boxed set of the work produced shortly after its first performances made the *War Requiem* unique as a postwar work of classical music. It was acclaimed almost universally as a masterpiece, while a few critics remained sniffy about the sheer degree of the brouhaha and publicity. Stravinsky, the greatest living composer himself, complained with a pun about the "Battle of Britten" atmosphere and withering comments about how audience members should be sure to bring with them a box of Kleenex tissues.[15]

Britten was made uncomfortable by the public success

of the *War Requiem* (as Stravinsky wrote, "nothing fails like success, or hurts more than the press's ready certification of a 'masterpiece'"[16]), and it brought an end to a certain period in his life as a public figure. He didn't compose any of his subsequent significant works in this publicly accessible manner. His musical style became more spiky, more modern. The church parables that followed throughout the decade, including *Curlew River*, were challengingly offbeat and idiosyncratic. He wrote some intimate chamber music (including cello sonatas for Rostropovich) and a television opera, *Owen Wingrave*, which has rather languished from neglect. The one really big piece he wrote was his last opera, *Death in Venice* (1973), based on the 1911 novella by Thomas Mann.

The story is a well known one.

The celebrated writer Gustav von Aschenbach is suffering from creative block. Taking a walk in his hometown, Munich, he enters a cemetery where he encounters a mysterious traveler whose appearance inspires him to travel to the south to break his imaginative logjam. He journeys to Venice, and while there becomes increasingly drawn to a young Polish boy, Tadzio, who is staying in the same hotel on the Venetian Lido. A cholera outbreak reaches Venice, and Aschenbach fails to warn Tadzio's family of the danger while at the same time delaying his own departure. Finally, Tadzio's family make arrangements to leave. Aschenbach dies—from the cholera, from a heart attack, from artistic exhaustion—as he watches Tadzio on the beach, fighting with another boy and then walking out to sea.

Biographical criticism has its dangers but remains endlessly tempting and, as far as I am concerned as a singer, often productive in coming to terms with the works that I seek to interpret. The autobiographical quality of both Thomas Mann and Benjamin Britten's engagement with Aschenbach's story has long been noted.

Almost all of the events that happen to Aschenbach on his way to and in Venice happened to Mann when he visited the city in the company of his family in 1911. The traveler in the Munich cemetery; the elderly rouged fop on board the Venice-bound ship; the engagement of a truculent gondolier on the way to the Hotel des Bains; the appearance of a fascinating Polish boy; the advent of cholera. The only difference is that Mann, of course, didn't stay in Venice to die.

Britten was endlessly drawn to Venice, as Edward Said puts it, "as a distant place to return to, and [in which] to locate or find . . . that immense reservoir of cultural memory contributed to by his predecessors."[17] But the city was also reportedly the scene of a crisis in Britten's life when, during the rehearsals for the premiere of his opera *The Turn of the Screw* at the Fenice opera house in 1952, he became dangerously obsessed with the young boy playing Miles in the opera, David Hemmings. This creates a link with the genesis of *Death in Venice* the novella, as Mann had been inspired to write the story partly by his own obsession with a boy in Venice when he holidayed there in 1911 with his wife. But, as with Mann, the obsession with the beauty of youth was only the beginning of a work that is much more complex and searching than its origins might suggest.

Britten's identification with Aschenbach was also broader than the issue of an inappropriate, potentially humiliating, and ultimately innocent attachment or obsession. It is clear in many passages of Aschenbach's self-analyzing, self-critical recitatives that run throughout the opera, none more so than this: "So I am led to Venice once again, egregio Signor von Aschenbach; the writer who has found a way to reconcile art and honours, the lofty purity of whose style has been officially recognised." There speaks the composer burned by the sheer success and popular acclaim of the *War Requiem*.

But I want to focus on another theme that really is at the heart of Britten's *Death in Venice*, obviously and incontestably—death, something he had been confronting in his music for some thirty-five years, from the *Sinfonia da Requiem* through the Donne sonnets to the *War Requiem*. The title of the work, *Death in Venice*, speaks for itself, but in Britten's case death was far more of a real presence as he composed the work than it had been for the thirty-five-year-old Thomas Mann, who wrote the novella as an exquisitely crafted exercise in autumnal imaginings. Britten postponed lifesaving, but also life-threatening, heart surgery—not ultimately successful—to compose the opera as a last gift for his lover and companion, Peter Pears. Britten's identification with Aschenbach may have been intense because of his own attraction to youth and because of his own creative struggles. But death is a recurring and insistent presence in the opera, even more so than in Mann's novella, as the multiple uncanny figures who unsettle Aschenbach's equilibrium—the traveler in the cemetery, the rouged and inebriated elderly fop on board ship, the gondolier with his coffin black gondola, and so on—are all played by a single singer-actor and hence unified into an almost medieval personification of death who leads Aschenbach in a macabre dance. The climax is reached in Aschenbach's dream in act 2, where baritone as Dionysius and countertenor as Apollo struggle for possession of the protagonist. Dionysius, with all his crucial epithets—the androgynous, the hidden, the liberator—is also a divine communicant between the living and the dead.

Before Aschenbach's final entrance in the last scene of

the opera, which ends with his death, slumped on the beach, the hotel manager—as played by the baritone—prepares for the departure of the guests with his assistant, the hotel porter. In one of the most chilling and uncanny moments in the whole opera, in response to the porter's query about Aschenbach, the manager replies, unaccompanied, "Be silent—who comes and goes is my affair." Suddenly the gulf between the timeless mythology of the dream, the dance of Dionysus, and the twentieth-century materiality of Venice's Grand Hotel des Bains closes, and in a startling moment of epiphanic force we see the hotel manager, in all his everyday banality, pomposity, and unctuousness, as death himself.

That moment is only amplified some bars later. A series of portentous remarks to Aschenbach himself carefully tread the boundary between the hotel world and the world of death: "Signore, it is the time of departures," "our work is nearly done." But then the manager removes the mask, singing these words: "No doubt the signore will be leaving us soon? We must all lose what we think to enjoy the most" (plate 4). He sings them to an easily recalled theme that has recurred throughout the opera and that was first introduced by the traveler in the cemetery at the beginning of the opera with the words "No boundaries hold you." The quasi-realistic, psychologistic surface of the opera slides away to reveal the abyss beneath. There is something extraordinarily moving and, in the end, supremely real about this elision of the quotidian and the eschatological, something on which those who have lived on the boundary between life and death can report.

There is a big difference between the thrust of Mann's story and of Britten's opera despite Britten's typical faithfulness to so much of the original material. Britten composed three operas based on classic novellas, and in all three cases—Herman

Melville's *Billy Budd*, Henry James's *The Turn of the Screw*, and *Death in Venice* itself—the original texts remain crucial guides in rehearsal. The dramatic logic of the music, as opposed to the bare bones of the libretto, is often clearly grounded in the original, literary text. Luchino Visconti's celebrated film of *Death in Venice* was made around the time Britten was getting to grips with his opera (creating all sorts of tricky copyright issues), and there is a striking contrast between Visconti's departure from the Mann original—reimagining Aschenbach as a composer above all—and Britten's imaginative engagement with the text.[18] But Britten's musical and theatrical presentation of Aschenbach does mean that Britten necessarily removes Mann's ironic narratological frame, the voice of the narrator that Mann manipulates in such a complex way. The opera has no place for an ironizing narrator. Instead Britten presents a mind onstage, a mind unveiled in Aschenbach's recitative soliloquies, a mind that we watch unraveling in the face of those Freudian twins, desire and death.

Death in Venice falls into a two-act structure, pivoting around an ominous sound, low in the orchestra, horns and double bass, on a sustained E and B.[19] This accompanies and is held for a very long pause after Aschenbach's lonely and tortured declaration of love for Tadzio. It's deeply reminiscent of the double bass drone that starts Tchaikovsky's "Pathetique" symphony, and the pitches are the same, E and B. The same drone commences the second act of the opera, which leads Aschenbach towards his inevitable demise. Britten had already quoted the "Pathetique" in the last movement of an earlier piece, his orchestral song cycle of 1958, the *Nocturne*. The "Pathetique" is notoriously a work drenched in presentiments of death as well as homosexual longing, the first performance led by the composer only nine days before his demise. Like Aschenbach, Tchaikovsky almost certainly died as the result of a cholera infection; and rumors abounded that it was an honor suicide connected to the composer's infatuation with a teenage boy.

⊢

There are two ways of ending this book with some music, but I am unsure as to which of two pieces to choose. Both are examples of the way in which music can calmly look death in the face and reach a sort of accommodation with it; both of them were written by a man facing death and for whom death had been a major theme through all of his compositional life. As farewells to life, they are both statements, if Delphic ones, about the identity of their composers; the last word but a word that remains resolutely undefined.

I could choose the bells from the last movement of Britten's last string quartet, his third, and the last major piece he completed before his death. That movement is titled "La Serenissima," and Britten wrote it in Venice. It opens with a recitative that contains five quotations from *Death in Venice*. It ends with a passacaglia based on a theme from the opera. The bell-like sounds of the cello in that concluding section hark back to those bells of John Donne's, a farewell to life. They are the bells of Venice, the bells Britten is listening to in a photograph from his last trip to the city, in November 1975, leaning on the balcony of his room in the Danieli Hotel, housed in the Palazzo Dandolo, where more than three centuries earlier, Monteverdi's *Combattimento* had first been performed.

But I'll end with *Death in Venice* itself, written a couple of years earlier.

This is a role I have performed in two productions: Deborah Warner's for the English National Opera in 1997 (a pro-

FIGURE 6. Benjamin Britten on the balcony of his room at the Hotel Danieli, Venice, November 1975. Photograph © William Servaes, 1975. Image provided by Britten Pears Arts (brittenpearsarts.org). Ref: PH/4/531.

duction in whose initiation and conception I was deeply involved), and Graham Vick's for the Deutsche Oper in 2019 (where I came in for a revival of a preexisting show). The two approaches could not, in a sense, have been more different, and not just in terms of costume and design—Warner's production was period, Vick's modern dress. In the Warner version, as in her 1997 realization of *The Turn of the Screw*, the director's approach was subtle and ambiguous: sexuality was not foregrounded. The orgiastic Bacchic dream that precedes Aschenbach's final descent into humiliation and death was staged as a scene of social stigmatization in which the dreamed disapproval of the guests of the Hotel des Bains drowns the sleeping Aschenbach in writhing, nightmarish embarrassment. Over the course of the whole opera, I experienced the force of Mann's tale and of Britten's opera as very much a parable about creativity and humiliation.

Vick's production in Berlin made Mann's sexual implications, projected through Britten's music drama, far more explicit. Boys lolled suggestively on the beach, Aschenbach put his hand on a strawberry seller's breast; there was coarser innuendo in the brilliantly theatrical traveling player's scene in the second act; there were explicit offers of sex in the street sellers' scene in the first. Ever since the musicologist Philip Brett opened up Britten's operas to readings grounded in his sexuality—a necessary liberation[20]—an emphasis on sex has sometimes obtruded, obscuring the other issues that inform Britten's work and underestimating the powerful expressive force of repression, which fuels the intensity of much of Britten's music. But at the same time one cannot deny the powerful force of sexuality in Britten's oeuvre from the beginning to the end: from the polymorphous sensuality of *Les illuminations*, settings of Rimbaud, dripping with longing but shot through with political foreboding (the work was completed in September 1939 as Poland fell to the Nazis), to the quivering eroticism of the dramatic cantata *Phaedra*, one of the composer's very last works, written in the same year as the third string quartet—"I want your sword's spasmodic final inch." What I found in returning to the opera in Vick's production a dozen years after my first assumption of the role was the closer presence of death. Maybe because Eros, death's Freudian twin, was uncomfortably, embarrassingly, disturbingly insistent. Or maybe because I was now closer to Gustav Aschenbach in age than to Thomas Mann, and had had, like Benjamin Britten, my own encounter with cardiac medicine, having experienced open heart surgery only a few months before. One of my doctors was a junior in the hospital where Britten was treated in the early 1970s; he remembered that the composer had a clavichord installed in his room.

⊢

Aschenbach is dead, or dying, in a deck chair on the Venetian Lido as Tadzio—a silent, danced role in the opera—walks far out to sea to the haunting accompaniment of shimmering rising and falling glockenspiel arpeggios embossed on a slow threnody from woodwinds, horns, and strings. It's a moment of sublime beauty which, despite all the desperation of the preceding action, despite the smell of death and carbolic hanging in the air, seems to represent a calm vision of life continuing, the young succeeding the old.

Acknowledgments

F irst and foremost I would like to thank Randy Berlin and her late husband Melvin for creating this visionary lecture series in a time of crisis for the humanities.

At the University of Chicago, many thanks to Anne W. Robertson, Sara Patterson, Berthold Hoeckner, and Martha Feldman.

At the University of Chicago Press I have been lucky to work with my editor Marta Tonegutti, with Kristin Rawlings, and to receive useful advice from two anonymous readers.

For help and inspiration of various sorts, and in no particular order, I would like to thank Manuel Cornejo; Catriona Seth; Deborah Warner; Netia Jones; Antonio Lysy; Alessio Bax; Lucille Chung; Christian Poltéra; Emmanuel Pahud; Ruby Philogene; Julius Drake; Fabio Biondi and Europa Galante; Harry Bicket, Angelika Kirchschlager and the English Concert; Charles Miller; Caroline Woodfield; Graham Johnson; and Nick Clark.

Most of all, thanks are due to Lucasta Miller, without whom . . .

Notes

Preface

1. The expressivity of the performer may also have been an offense against a Stravinskian aesthetic, one that the composer summed up, with typical provocation, in 1935: "I consider that music is, by its very nature, essentially powerless to express anything at all, whether a feeling, an attitude of mind, or psychological mood, a phenomenon of nature, etc. . . . Expression has never been an inherent property of music. That is by no means the purpose of its existence." Igor Stravinsky, *An Autobiography* (London: Calder and Boyars, 1975), 53.
2. Heinrich Schenker, *The Art of Performance*, ed. Heribert Esser, trans. Irene Schreier Scott (Oxford: Oxford University Press, 2000), 3.
3. See especially Nicholas Cook, *Beyond the Score: Music as Performance* (New York: Oxford University Press, 2014).
4. Alfred Brendel, "Musical Character(s) in Beethoven's Piano Sonatas," in *On Music: Collected Essays* (Chicago: A Capella, 2001), 71.
5. Edward T. Cone, *The Composer's Voice* (Berkeley: University of California Press, 1974), 22–23.
6. Friedrich Nietzsche, *Menschliches, Allzumenschliches: Ein Buch für freie Geister* (Chemnitz: E. Schmeitzner, 1878), pt. 2, §171.

Chapter One

1. From the separate preface to *Combattimento* in the continuo part of the eighth book of madrigals, published in 1638.

2. Torquato Tasso, *Jerusalem Delivered*, ed. and trans. Anthony M. Esolen (Baltimore: Johns Hopkins University Press, 2000), 60, 242, 243.

3. Wendy Heller, *Emblems of Eloquence: Opera and Women's Voices in Seventeenth-Century Venice* (Berkeley: University of California Press, 2003).

4. Heller, 37.

5. James Aske's *Elizabeth triumphans* (1588), cited by Winfried Schleiner, "'Divine Virago': Queen Elizabeth as an Amazon," *Studies in Philology* 75, no. 2 (Spring 1978): 170.

6. Tasso's views on gender in both the *Gerusalemme liberata* and *Il discorso della virtù feminile e donnesca* are discussed in Gerry Milligan, *Moral Combat: Women, Gender, and War in Italian Renaissance Literature* (Toronto: University of Toronto Press, 2018), esp. 66 and 209.

7. See Eric R. Dursteler's fascinating *Renegade Women: Gender, Identity, and Boundaries in the Early Modern Mediterranean* (Baltimore: Johns Hopkins University Press, 2011).

8. Suzanne G. Cusick, "'Indarno chiedi': Clorinda and the Interpretation of Monteverdi's *Combattimento*," in *Word, Image, Song: Essays on Early Modern Italy*, ed. Rebecca Cypess, Beth Lise Glixon, and Nathan Link (Rochester, NY: University of Rochester Press, 2013), 136–38.

9. On this cadence and the importance of location for the meanings of the piece, see Antonio Cascelli, "Place, Performance and Identity in Monteverdi's *Combattimento di Tancredi e Clorinda*," *Cambridge Opera Journal* 29, no. 2 (2018): 177–86.

10. Charles Rosen, *The Romantic Generation* (Cambridge, MA: Harvard University Press, 1995), 115.

11. Kristina Muxfeldt, "*Frauenliebe und Leben*: Now and Then," *19th Century Music* 25, no. 1 (Summer 2001): 27–48.

12. Rufus Hallmark, "*Frauenliebe und Leben*": *Chamisso's Poems and Schumann's Songs* (Cambridge: Cambridge University Press, 2014).

13. For the traditional view of the persona in *Frauenliebe*, see Edward T. Cone, *The Composer's Voice* (Berkeley: University of California Press, 1974), 23: "We accept the performance of *Dichterliebe* by a woman, but not of *Frauenliebe* by a man—although we would permit a man to sing a narrative in which a woman's voice is quoted. The singer is the actual, living embodiment of the vocal protagonist—he is the persona turned into a person; and we insist on a modicum of congruence within the framework of our usual stage conventions."

14. Quoted in Dietrich Fischer-Dieskau, *Robert Schumann: Words and Music* (Portland, OR: Amadeus Press, 1988), 89.

15. It was Baudelaire who first analyzed the blurred gender of Flaubert's heroine:

> Il ne restait plus à l'auteur, pour accomplir le tour de force dans son entier, que de se dépouiller (autant que possible) de son sexe et de se faire femme. Il en est résulté une merveille; c'est que, malgré

tout son zèle de comédien, il n'a pas pu ne pas infuser un sang viril dans les veines de sa créature, et que madame Bovary, pour ce qu'il y a en elle de plus énergique et de plus ambitieux, et aussi de plus rêveur, madame Bovary est restée un homme. Comme la Pallas armée, sortie du cerveau de Zeus, ce bizarre androgyne a gardé toutes les séductions d'une âme virile dans un charmant corps féminin.

Selected Critical Studies of Baudelaire, ed. Douglas Parmée (Cambridge: Cambridge University Press, 1949), 73–74.

16. Quoted in Nancy B. Reich, *Clara Schumann: The Artist and the Woman*, rev. ed. (Ithaca, NY: Cornell University Press, 2001), 87.

17. Reich, 63, 68–69.

18. *The Marriage Diaries of Robert and Clara Schumann: From Their Wedding Day through the Russian Trip*, ed. Gerd Nauhaus, trans. Peter Ostwald (Boston: Northeastern University Press, 1994).

19. Reich, *Clara Schumann*, 78.

20. Reich, 59.

21. Cited in Muxfeldt, "*Frauenliebe und Leben*: Now and Then," 36.

22. See Ivan Hewett, "I Understand How to Be a Woman," *Daily Telegraph*, April 13, 2006; and Matthew Gurewitsch, "Why Shouldn't Men Sing Romantic Drivel, Too?," *New York Times*, November 6, 2005.

23. Lawrence Kramer suggests that mid-nineteenth-century performance conventions were less prescriptive than those that developed from the late nineteenth century on: "This rigidity is symptomatic of the accelerating rise of modernity, which by disrupting traditional gender roles provoked a persistent anxiety about them. Modernity in its twentieth-century form was constantly haunted by the specters of disfigured gender." "Sexing Song: Brigitte Fassbaender's *Winterreise*," in *Word and Music Studies: Essays on Performativity and on Surveying the Field*, Word and Music Studies 12, ed. Walter Bernhart (Amsterdam: Rodopi, 2011), 157.

24. Quotation from *The Noh Drama: Ten Plays from the Japanese* (Rutland, VT: C.E. Tuttle, 1955), as used by Britten and Plomer, cited in Mikiko Ishii, "The Weeping Mothers in *Sumidagawa*, *Curlew River*, and Medieval European Religious Plays," *Comparative Drama* 39, no. 3/4 (Fall/Winter 2005–2006): 290.

25. *Britten on Music*, ed. Paul Francis Kildea (Oxford: Oxford University Press, 2003), 381–82.

26. See the groundbreaking study by Heather Wiebe, *Britten's Unquiet Pasts: Sound and Memory in Postwar Reconstruction* (Cambridge: Cambridge University Press, 2012).

27. Wiebe.

28. *The English Auden: Poems, Essays, and Dramatic Writing, 1927–1939*, ed. Edward Mendelson (London: Faber and Faber, 1986), 341–42.

29. Humphrey Carpenter, *Benjamin Britten: A Biography* (New York: Charles Scribner's Sons, 1992), 436.

30. Brett's influential essays are collected in his *Music and Sexuality in Britten: Selected Essays*, ed. George E. Haggerty (Berkeley: University of California Press, 2006).

31. Cited in Frank Episale, "Gender, Tradition, and Culture in Translation: Reading the 'Onnagata' in English," *Asian Theatre Journal* 29, no. 1 (Spring 2012): 93, emphasis mine.

Chapter Two

The epigraph is from Walter Benjamin, "Theses on the Philosophy of History VII," in *Illuminations*, trans. Harry Zohn (London: Jonathan Cape, 1970).

1. Antonio Gramsci, *Selections from The Prison Notebooks*, trans. and ed. Quintin Hoare and Geoffrey Nowell-Smith (London: Lawrence and Wishart, 1971), 324. The original is in Antonio Gramsci, *Quaderni del carcere: 2*, ed. Valentino Gerratana (Turin: Einaudi, 1975), 1376: "L'inizio del elaborazione critica è la coscienza di quello che è realmente, cioè un 'conosci te stesso' come prodotto del processo storico finora svoltosi che ha lasciato in te stesso un'infinità di tracce accolte senza beneficio d'inventario."

2. Ralph P. Locke, *Musical Exoticism: Images and Reflections* (Cambridge: Cambridge University Press, 2009), and *Music and the Exotic from the Renaissance to Mozart* (Cambridge: Cambridge University Press, 2015).

3. Solofo Randrianja and Stephen Ellis, *Madagascar: A Short History* (London: Hurst, 2009), 75. For a different view, see Gwyn Campbell, *An Economic History of Imperial Madagascar, 1750–1895: The Rise and Fall of an Island Empire* (New York: Cambridge University Press, 2005).

4. Sonia E. Howe, *The Drama of Madagascar* (London: Methuen, 1938), 11, 15.

5. Howe, 28.

6. Howe, 32.

7. Étienne de Flacourt, *Histoire de la Grande Isle Madagascar* (Paris: Luyne, 1658); new edition, annotated, augmented, and introduced by Claude Allibet (Paris: Karthala, 2007).

8. Sonia Howe's *Drama of Madagascar* provides a readable and detailed if somewhat dated account of the abortive expeditions. For more recent studies, see, for example, Pier M. Larson, "Colonies Lost: God, Hunger, and Conflict in Anosy (Madagascar) to 1674," *Comparative Studies of South Asia, Africa and the Middle East* 27, no. 2 (2007): 345–66; Denis Regnier and Dominique Somda, "Slavery and Post-Slavery in Madagascar: An Overview," in *African Islands: Leading Edges of Empire and Globalization*, ed. Toyin Falola, Danielle Porter Sanchez, and R. Joseph Parrott (Rochester, NY: University of Rochester Press, 2019), 345–69; Mike Parker Pearson, "Close Encounters of the Worst Kind: Malagasy Resistance and Colonial Disasters in Southern Madagascar," *World Archaeology* 28, no. 3 (February 1997): 393–417. See also G. S. P. Freeman-Grenville, *The French at Kilwa Island: An Episode in 18th-Century*

East African History (Oxford: Clarendon, 1965) for the Sieur Morice's scheme (1777) for "a French commercial empire . . . stretching from the Mascarenes to the Swahili and Mozambique coast, in which Madagascar would play a central part" (Campbell, *Economic History*, 6). The French government rejected the scheme in 1779.

9. See the excellent online resource of the Plantation Society at https:// www.portail-esclavage-reunion.fr/en/documentaires/plantation-society /historical-context/. See also Albert Jauze, "Malgaches et Africains à Bourbon: La Réunion à l'époque de l'esclavage," *Hommes et migrations*, no. 1275 (September/October 2008): 150–57.

10. Thomas Piketty, *Capital and Ideology* (Cambridge, MA: Harvard University Press, 2020), 213–17.

11. Plantation Society, https://www.portail-esclavage-reunion.fr/en/ documentaires/plantation-society/historical-context/.

12. On Parny, see Catriona Seth's definitive biography, *Évariste Parny (1753–1814): Créole, révolutionnaire, académicien* (Paris: Hermann, 2014), and *Selected Poetry and Prose of Évariste Parny in English Translation, with French Text*, ed. Françoise Lionnet, trans. Peter Low and Blake. Smith (New York: Modern Language Association of America, 2018).

13. Lionnet, 184.

14. Lionnet, 161.

15. Noro Rakotobe-d'Alberto, "L'univers culturel malgache dans les *Chansons Madécasses d'Évariste Parny*," in *Lumières et océan Indien: Bernardin de Saint-Pierre, Évariste Parny, Antoine de Bertin*, ed. C. Meure and G. Armand (Paris: Classiques Garnier, 2017), 67–84.

16. Seth, *Évariste Parny (1753–1814)*, 81.

17. Lionnet, *Selected Poetry and Prose of Évariste Parny*, 165.

18. Lionnet, 165.

19. For a more heroic, less complex view of Parny's opposition to slavery, see Edward D. Seeber, "Parny as an Opponent of Slavery," *Modern Language Notes* 49, no. 6 (June 1934): 360–66.

20. Étienne de Flacourt, *Histoire de la Grande Isle Madagascar* (Paris: Luyne, 1658); new edition, annotated, augmented, and introduced by Claude Allibet (Paris: Karthala, 2007), 645. The translation is mine.

21. Jean-Michel Racault, "'Méfiez-vous des blancs, habitants du rivage': Anti-colonialisme et intertextualité dans les *Chansons Madécasses* de Parny," in *Apprendre à porter sa vue au loin: Hommage à Michèle Duchet*, ed. Sylviane Albertan-Coppola (Lyon: ENS, 2009), 306.

22. Frantz Fanon, *The Wretched of the Earth*, trans. Constance Farrington (Harmondsworth: Penguin Books, 1967), 28, 73, 74; originally published as *Les damnés de la terre* (Paris: François Maspero, 1961).

23. In exchange, the French gave the British a free hand in Zanzibar; see Campbell, *Economic History*, 4.

24. See Randrianja and Ellis, *Madagascar*, 123–59.

25. There has been some confusion about the date of this premiere. With scrupulous attention to contemporary press reports, Manuel Cornejo (editor of Maurice Ravel, *L'intégrale: Correspondence (1895–1937), écrits et entretiens* [Paris: Le Passeur, 2018]) has established the performance history of the *Chansons madécasses*, arguing that the premiere was on May 25, 1925, and not, as some accounts have maintained, in October. See *Paris-Midi*, May 29, 1925, https://dezede.org/sources/id/70735/.

26. Arthur Hoerée, "*Chanson madécasse*, par M. Ravel (Soirée Mrs Coolidge)," *La revue musicale* 6, no. 11 (October 1925): 243–44; "L'oeuvre vocale," in "Hommage à Maurice Ravel," special issue, *La revue musicale* 19, no. 187 (December 1938): 102–9, 294–301. On Ravel and the exotic, see also Stephen Zank, *Irony and Sound: The music of Maurice Ravel* (Rochester, NY: University of Rochester Press, 2009), and Federico Lazzaro, "*Chansons madécasses*, modernisme et érotisme: Pour une écoute de Ravel au-delà de l'exotisme," in "Musique et exotisme en France au tournant du XXe siècle: Altérités recomposées," ed. Sylvain Caron, *Revue Musicale OIRCM* 3, no. 1 (2016).

27. "A Visit with Maurice Ravel," *De Telegraaf*, March 31, 1931, 472–75.

28. Roland-Manuel, *Hommage à Maurice Ravel* (Paris: La revue musicale1938); translated as *Maurice Ravel* by Cynthia Jolly (London: D. Dobson, 1947), 95–96.

29. "L'oignon demande un sol épais et gras; / Un sol léger suffit à la semence; / Confiez-lui votre douce espérance / Et de vos fleurs les germes délicats." Roland-Manuel, *Maurice Ravel*, trans. Cynthia Jolly (London: D. Dobson), 96.

30. Roland-Manuel, *Maurice Ravel*, trans. Jolly, 95–96.

31. Manuel Rosenthal, *Ravel: Souvenirs de Manuel Rosenthal*, ed. Marcel Marnat (Paris: Hazan, 1995), 127.

32. Cited by Jane. F. Fulcher in her *The Composer as Intellectual: Music and Ideology in France 1914–1940*, (New York: Oxford University Press, 2005), 67. She, and from an opposed perspective, Steven Huebner, give the fullest accounts of Ravel's politics. See Steven Huebner, "Ravel's Politics," *Musical Quarterly* 97, no. 1 (Spring 2014): 66–97.

33. Fulcher, *The Composer as Intellectual*, 137.

34. David Drake, "The PCF, the Surrealists, Clarté and the Rif War," *French Cultural Studies* 17, no. 2 (2006): 173–88. See also David H. Slavin, "The French Left and the Rif War, 1924–25: Racism and the Limits of Internationalism," *Journal of Contemporary History* 26, no. 1 (January 1991): 5–32.

35. Cited in Jonathan G. Katz, "The 1907 Mauchamp Affair and the French Civilising Mission in Morocco," *Journal of North African Studies* 6, no. 1 (2011): 145.

36. From Parny, "Il est doux," third song of Ravel's *Chansons madécasses*.

37. Fulcher, *The Composer as Intellectual*, 144.

38. Richard James discusses the extent to which Ravel may have used Malagasy models in his cycle in an important but inconclusive article, "Ravel's 'Chansons Madécasses': Ethnic Fantasy or Ethnic Borrowing?," *Musical Quarterly* 74, no. 3 (1990): 360–84.

39. See Graham Johnson, *Poulenc: The Life in the Songs* (New York: Liveright, 2020), 13–14.
40. Petrine Archer-Straw, *Negrophilia: Avant-Garde Paris and Black Culture in the 1920s* (New York: Thames and Hudson, 2000), 58.
41. *The Oxford Dictionary of American Quotations*, ed. Hugh Rawson and Margaret Miner, 2nd ed. (Oxford: Oxford University Press, 2006), 567.
42. Archer-Straw, *Negrophilia*, 38. See also Andy Fry, *Paris Blues: African American Music and French Popular Culture, 1920–1960* (Chicago: University of Chicago Press, 2014).
43. Telephone conversation and email exchange with Ruby Philogene. For the possible origins of Ravel's "Aoua" in Julien Tiersot's exoticizing description of the cries of Malagasy visitors (captives? colonial exhibits?) at the Paris World Exhibition of 1889 in his chapter on African music in the *Encyclopédie de la musique et dictionnaire de conservatoire* (1922), see Stephen Zank, *Irony and Sound: The Music of Maurice Ravel* (Rochester, NY: University of Rochester Press, 2009), 207–8.
44. *Marx and Engels: Basic Writings on Politics and Philosophy*, ed. Lewis S. Feuer (London: Collins, 1969), 360.

Chapter Three

1. Bernard Williams, "The Makropulos Case: Reflections on the Tedium of Immortality," in *Problems of the Self: Philosophical Papers, 1956–1972* (Cambridge: Cambridge University Press, 1973), 82–100.
2. George Steiner, *Real Presences* (Chicago: University of Chicago Press, 1989), 226. Perhaps the scene in J. M. Coetzee's *Summertime* in which he persuades his girlfriend to have sex with him to the accompaniment of the quintet's slow movement is a comical reproach to such a reading and at the same time a confirmation of it: "[He] wanted us to co-ordinate our activities to the music. . . . [It] may be very beautiful but I found it far from arousing." Originally published 2009 and reprinted in his *Scenes from Provincial Life* (London: Harvill Secker, 2011), 337.
3. Humphrey Carpenter, *Benjamin Britten: A Biography* (London: Faber and Faber, 1992), 145–47; Paul Kildea, *Benjamin Britten: A Life in the Twentieth Century* (London: Allen Lane, 2013), 160, 169–71.
4. For the account of Britten's trip to Germany I draw on Kildea, *Benjamin Britten*, 253–57; Carpenter, *Benjamin Britten*, 226–28; Justin Vickers, "Benjamin Britten's Silent 'Epilogue' to 'The holy sonnets of John Donne,'" *Musical Times* 156, no. 1933 (Winter 2015): 17–30. Britten's familiarity with Donne's verse was encouraged by his friend W. H. Auden. In 1941 he made an incomplete sketch for voice and piano of Donne's "Stay, O Sweet and Do Not Rise"; towards the end of his life he realized Pelham Humfrey's seventeenth-century setting of Donne's "Hymn to God the Father."

5. "Death's Duell," in *The Works of John Donne* (London: John W. Parker, 1839), 6:279.

6. "Ben and I have been re-reading Donne lately—those wonderful holy sonnets, and especially the Hymn to God the Father"; Pears to Elizabeth Mayer, February 13, 1943; see *Letters from a Life: Selected Letters and Diaries of Benjamin Britten*, ed. Donald Mitchell, Philip Reed, Rosamund Strode, Kathleen Mitchell, and Judy Young (London: Faber, 1991), 2:1277.

7. *The Complete English Poems of John Donne*, ed. C.A. Patrides (London: Dent, 1985), stanza 3, p. 490.

8. John Carey, *John Donne: Life, Mind and Art*, new ed. (London: Faber and Faber, 1990), 186. One of Donne's greatest fears was the loss of identity that death involves. In his sermon he imagines a "private and *retir'd man*, that thought himself his owne for ever" who loses himself, as Ramie Targoff puts it, "within the collective mass of the dead": "This is the most inglorious and contemptible *vilification*, the most deadly and peremptory *nullification* of man, that we can consider . . . in this death of *incineration*, and dispersal of dust, we see *nothing* that we can call *that mans*." See Ramie Targoff, "Facing Death," in *The Cambridge Companion to John Donne*, ed. Achsah Guibbory (Cambridge: Cambridge University Press, 2006), 227–28.

9. *The Complete English Poems of John Donne*, ed. C.A. Patrides (London: Dent, 1985), 434.

10. Carey, *John Donne*, 185.

11. On this epilogue, see the extensive exploration by Vickers, "Benjamin Britten's silent 'Epilogue.'"

12. *Devotions upon Emergent Occasions, together with Death's Duell* (Ann Arbor: University of Michigan Press, 1959), 109.

13. I performed this song as an encore at the Wigmore Hall with pianist Julius Drake during the early stages of the second Iraq War. The audience silence after the song had finished was more intense than any I can remember.

14. *The Poems of Wilfred Owen*, ed. with a memoir by Edmund Blunden (London: Chatto and Windus, 1955), 179.

15. Igor Stravinsky and Robert Craft, *Themes and Conclusions* (London: Faber and Faber, 1972), 26–27.

16. Stravinsky and Craft.

17. Edward W. Said, *On Late Style* (London: Bloomsbury, 2006).

18. See T.J. Reed, *Death in Venice: Making and Unmaking a Master* (New York: Twayne, 1994), 20, and Philip Kitcher, *Deaths in Venice: The Cases of Gustav von Aschenbach* (New York: Columbia University Press, 2013), 102–7 and 109–12.

19. This is a rare case where a librettist, in this case Myfanwy Piper, had stronger instincts and a better sense of what the composer intended than did Britten himself. Worrying about the length of the opera and the balance between acts one and two, Britten had suggested resorting to a three-act structure.

In a long letter, "Mrs Piper carefully argued the dramatic and practical issues involved from a number of standpoints, and this crucial question was not to be resolved until the end of the year." Piper "argued that Aschenbach's declaration of love for Tadzio at the end of the present Act I was preceded by a gradual build-up, and followed in Act II by a 'downward rush . . . to the inevitable end." After a playthrough on New Year's Eve 1972, Britten made the decision to stick to a two-act form and to place the caesura here. One cannot help thinking that the decision had already been made in the music and that Britten's ill health was, as it had with other issues surrounding the opera, making him untypically indecisive. *Letters from a Life: The Selected Letters of Benjamin Britten*, vol. 6, *1966–1976*, ed. P. Reed and M. Cooke (Woodbridge: Boydell Press, 2012), 534, 542.

20. Philip Brett, *Music and Sexuality in Britten* (Berkeley: University of California Press, 2006), 156.

Index

Page numbers in italics refer to illustrations; pl. *denotes a color plate.*

Britten, Benjamin (*continued*)
100n6, 100–101n19; Aschenbach, identification with, 83–84, 86; *Billy Budd*, 85–86; *Burning Fiery Furnace, The*, 26; *Canticle Two: Abraham and Isaac*, 22; *Ceremony of Carols*, 21–22; as conscientious objector, 68; *Curlew River*, 1–2, 17, 19–23, 25, 27–29, 82, *pl. 2*; death, theme of, 84; *Death in Venice*, 23, 82–89, *pl. 4*; *Holy Sonnets of John Donne, The*, 69, 71, 75–77, 81; "La Serenissima," 87; *Les illuminations*, 23, 89; *Midsummer Night's Dream, A*, 26; *Nocturne*, 86; oeuvre, sexuality in, 89; *Owen Wingrave* (with Piper), 82; as pacifist, 65, 79; *Peter Grimes*, 67; *Phaedra*, 89; public and private vision of death, elision of, 75; *Rape of Lucretia*, 21; *Serenade for Tenor, Horn and Strings*, 67; *Seven Sonnets of Michelangelo*, 67, 69; *Sinfonia da Requiem*, 65–67; *Sumidagawa*, 19, 22, 25; *Turn of the Screw, The*, 23, 83, 85–86, 88; *War Requiem*, 75, 77, 79–82, 84; *Who Are These Children?*, 79–80
Burning Fiery Furnace, The (Britten), 26
Byles, Edward, *26*

Cage, John, *4'33"*, 62
Canticle Two: Abraham and Isaac (Britten), 22
Carey, John, 71, 73–74
Carlyle, Joan, *26*
carnival, 2–3, 7; and gender confusion, 16
Carpenter, Humphrey, 23, 25
castrato, 16
Cavaye, Ronald, 27
Ceremony of Carols (Britten), 21–22
Chagrin, Claude, 27
Chamisso, Adelbert von, 11
Chansons madécasses (Parny), 40,

42, 44, 48; "Aoua," 59; indigenous point of view, adoption of, 47; "Méfiez vous des blancs" (Beware the whites), 39, 43, 45–47, 49, 56–57
Chansons madécasses (Songs of Madagascar or Malagasy Songs) (Ravel), xiii, xviii, 32, 37, 39, 54, 58, 98n25; anticolonialism of, 35, 56–57; "Aoua," 50–52, 56, 59–60; "Asie," 52; attitude toward, 33; exotic, notion of, 34; "Les fleurs," 52; "L'indifférent," 52; as political statement, 34, 55–56; "Zanahang and Niang," 44
Chester cycle (mystery plays), 22
Chicago Symphony Orchestra, 80
"Children, The" (Soutar), 79–80
China, 66
Chung, Lucille, 60
classical music, xi–xii, xvii, 32, 34, 81; classical music theater, 28; classical singers, xv; finality, engagement with, 63; ideal interpretation, as noninterpretation, xiv; musical score, xiv; natural delivery, as myth, xv; text, privileging of, xiv
Coetzee, J. M., *Summertime*, 99n2
colonialism, 34, 55, 58
Cone, Edward T., xvi
Congo, 53, 55
Congress of Berlin, 48
Coolidge, Elizabeth Sprague, 49–51
Copland, Aaron, 50
Cornejo, Manuel, 98n25
Coventry Cathedral, 77, 79
COVID-19 pandemic, xi–xii
Curlew River (Britten), 20–22, *24*, 82; blurring of gender, 1, 2, 28–29; cross-dressing casting, 25; gender and identity, 23; gender reversal, 17; Noh plays, inspired by, 17, 19, 25–27; October 2014 US premiere, *pl. 2*; performativity of theater, 27
Cusick, Suzanne, 8